ROLLING OUR OWN
Women as printers, publishers and distributors

Eileen Cadman
Gail Chester
Agnes Pivot

MINORITY
PRESS·GROUP

9 Poland Street · London W1V 3DG · Tel: 01-437 8954

The **Minority Press Group** was set up to investigate and monitor the radical media in Britain today. The aim of the project is to provide basic information, investigate problem areas, share the experiences of those working within the radical media and to encourage debate about its future development.

Rolling Our Own was commissioned by the **Minority Press Group** and written by Eileen Cadman, Gail Chester and Agnes Pivot.

Missing from acknowledgments:
Cambridge Women's Liberation Newsletter
Women In Print

First published in 1981 by:
Minority Press Group, 9 Poland Street, London W1V 3DG
Telephone: 01-437 8954

© Minority Press Group and Eileen Cadman, Gail Chester and Agnes Pivot
ISBN 0 906 890 071 (paper)
ISBN 0 906 890 063 (hard)

Design & layout
Marjo Xeridat
Printed by
Women In Print, 16A Iliffe Yd. off Crampton street, London SE17
(01 701 8314)
Cover printed by
Expression Printers Ltd, London N7
(01-607 4538)
Typeset by
Dark Moon, 43 All Saints Road, London W11
(01-221 4331)
Trade Distribution by
Southern Distribution, Albion Yard, Balfe Street, London N1
(01-837 1460)
Scottish & Northern Distribution, 4th Floor, 18 Granby Row, Manchester M13 (061-228 3903)
Scottish & Northern Distribution, 45/7 Niddry Street, Edinburgh EH1 1KG (031-557 0133)

Contents

Acknowledgements

Thank you:

To Jennifer Beerbohm, Jackie Lebe and Julie Armstrong for typing the interviews.
To Jay Dixon for editing the manuscript.
To Majo Xeridat for designing it.
To Dark Moon for typesetting it.
And to Women in Print for printing it.
To Amanda Sebestyen for pushing us to start this project and to Dave Morley and Charles Landry for pushing us to finish it.
To all those who agreed to be interviewed or who wrote to us to give their views and criticisms:
Onlywomen Press
Moss Side Community Press Women's Co-op
Jo Somerset
Lesley Merryfinch
The Women's Press
Virago Press
Stramullion
Sheba Feminist Publishers
Red Lion Setters
Dark Moon Typesetters
Jo Nesbitt
Sheila Rowbotham
Diana Leonard
Caryl Churchill
WRRC
Maggie Walker of Grass Roots Books
Sisterwrite Bookshop
Anne McDermid
Jay Dixon
Majo Xeridat
Jan Childs of Lambeth Library Services
Licking the Bed Clean Collective
m/f
Feminist Review
Catcall
Carolyn Brown of *WEA Women's Studies Newsletter*
Spare Rib
Esther Hodge of *Women Speaking*
Gay Jones
Elizabeth Bargh of the Printing and Publishing Industry Training Board
Brenda Philbin of the National Graphical Association
Sue Ledwith
Felicity Hunt
Ann Onymus

Introduction

This book is not based on statistics but on experience, our own as well as the women we are writing about. We have concentrated more on the initiatives of women who have established their own enterprises, and less on those who are fighting to work on equal terms with men in established workplaces, whether it is in a printing works or a typesetting firm.

Women have always had an important place in publishing. This industry is unlike many others in that women are heaped not only at the bottom of the job hierarchy but also in the middle. This makes them appear comparatively powerful but nevertheless, the number of women with real power at the top is negligible.

We think that struggling within existing workplaces and establishing autonomous women's ventures are both very important, but the aim of this book is to encourage women to realise that they can do things themselves. Therefore nearly all of the women we've interviewed are feminists. A few don't call themselves feminists but we interviewed them because we thought their work valuable, but without the women's movement, the impetus would not have existed for most of us.

When the Minority Press Group asked us to write this book (it started as a pamphlet!) we wanted to show how feminism was experienced by the groups we interviewed, how and why they decided to be autonomous. After doing the interviews it became clear that the main themes apart from feminism were money and men. This may sound like a cheap thriller, but it reflects the feeling of most women that their motivation for starting was their feminism, which made them question their working relationship with men in this society and that without financial control it is impossible to succeed in developing a feminist enterprise.

The notion of collective working appears throughout the book as it is a crucial practice of the Women's Liberation Movement. Although we believe that it is only by dismantling hierarchical relationships and sharing skills that we will achieve change, we are also conscious of the difficulties of working in collectives and its disadvantages (My God, the slowness of it all!).

Since we spend the whole book talking about other collectives perhaps we should say a few words about ours. We encountered both the difficulties and joys of working in such a set-up. Between us we have experienced all the areas we discuss in this book except for type-setting and printing. Each chapter had its own problems, some of which we solved, others we didn't because they were often a matter of opinion. When we sent the finished chapters to the women concerned, comments were varied and sometimes contradictory to one another. We did not always agree with what the others had written; sometimes we had to agree to differ, at other times we ended up with compromise.

Some days we became utterly fed up with the work and with each other, but at other times the feeling of working collectively was exhilarating; so this book is dedicated to the Women's Liberation Movement with love and frustration.

1
WOMEN WRITERS
AND
THE INFLUENCE
OF FEMINISM

'Women writers' is a very broad term. It covers women who are journal-ists, academics, romance writers, 'serious' fiction writers, and so on. We have deliberately chosen a variety of women from across these categ-ories to try and show how feminism has affected their approach and attitudes to their work, and how certain issues are common to them, despite the differences in the forms of expression they use.

Sheila Rowbotham is a feminist who is well known in the British Women's Liberation Movement (WLM) and abroad for her political writings and her contributions to women's history. She has a two-year-old son, and lives communally with several other people. Caryl Churchill is a playwright who has had her plays produced on radio, television and the stage, the latter mainly by fringe groups. She is married and lives with her husband and three sons. Diana Leonard is a sociologist, with a lectureship at the Institute of Education in London, and currently working on a women's studies course at the Open University. She is active in the WLM and lives with her three children and three other adults.

One of the results of the growth of the WLM has been the experi-ments made in different ways of working, to reduce the isolation of the writer and provide support structures. We spoke to the poetry collective who wrote and produced their own booklet of their poems and draw-ings called *Licking the Bed Clean*. They are a mixture of women, some with children, others without.

CALL YOURSELF A WRITER?

One of the questions we put to the women was: do you see yourself as 'a writer'? This may seem a rather strange question, and not one which you would address to a male writer. Why then is the issue of identity a question for women?

There are several aspects to this question which do not resolve them-selves into a single answer. The main reason which prevents women identifying themselves as 'professionals' and therefore adopting the label of 'writer' is the economic one. In our society you are identifiable as something when you earn money doing it, when you 'make your living' at it. Women earn their living by writing only relatively infrequently in comparison to men, hence the idea that there are fewer women writers.

Sheila and Caryl both had something to say about the question of identity:

Sheila: "I had always been writing. I wrote letters at great length and poems. I've only just started to really think of myself as a writer, because I used to think of myself as a person who was teaching and happened to write. I had been writing my thesis that never got finished because I wrote it a third too long. Also, my background taught me that people were not writers, so I had a sort of resistance to seeing myself as a writer. I do now though, because I am completely financially dependent on it."

But even though she does now earn her living by writing, she is still reluctant to perceive it in those terms, since her main motivation is political not economic:

"I'm not particularly enterprising in that I have no literary agent or anything like that, partly because I have a block to writing for money. If I really thought I was writing only for money I would completely dry up. I need the money, and I'm fairly willing to adapt what I write to make it something that can be marketed if it means that I could survive through it, but I could not just write something as a job."

Caryl talked of another factor which makes many women reluctant to classify themselves as writers by profession, lack of confidence:

"You get a woman who has been writing all her life but has not got the confidence to say she is a writer . . . I did not like to tell people that I was a writer even when I was at university, I did not like to formulate it. I was afraid of failing."

The women from the writing collective also talked about the question of identity. Stef Pixner wrote:

"Maybe the most important thing has been the way we've backed up each other's identities as *writers*. But thinking of myself that way made a big difference in setting up and keeping to a routine, making the time and the space and the priority."

Tina Reid:

"It does make a huge difference to me to have the group there. In a sense it makes me a writer. I don't mean I wouldn't write without it. But showing pieces to the group somehow turns them into something concrete and separate from me . . . And that changes my attitude towards the work, makes me feel I have a responsibility to say it as well and unambiguously as I possibly can."

Except for Sheila, none of the women live off their writing at present; all of them are trying to work out an identity as a writer in spite of this, and some have got further than others. The basis of this identity is not economic, they are not principally trying to reach the supposed nirvana of living off their writing, or sell a million copies of what they write. They are writing in order to raise certain political and ideological issues and to get these discussed. We can contrast this approach with that of a writer like Sara Harrison, author of a 'best-seller' called *Flowers of the Field*:

"The sums mentioned make your eyes bulge out like organ stops, and so obviously one begins to get greedy, I didn't used to be, but I am now, and I would certainly hope to make my million."

(Quoted in 'The Hype', *The Risk Business*, BBC TV 14.5.80.)

Sara Harrison was producing something that the publishers, agents and so on thought would sell; the women we are talking with are in a different league, with totally different motivations. They write out of themselves for political reasons, not according to tried and tested formulas.

TIME, GENTLEMEN, PLEASE!

The problem of making time to write has traditionally been more of a problem for women than for men — women don't normally have wives to look after the nitty-gritty of everyday life. Sheila said:

"I tend to be happiest when I can write, my main problem in my life is finding the space to do it. . . . To write about something that you've got to get into you need an amazing amount of time. It's no chance that academic blokes in universities, not involved in childcare and things are able to get on with it. . . . It's been hard to adjust to having Will, who's two. Before, I could carry on working until two in the morning. I can't now. . . . That's a big change."

Caryl also had to write in the odd few hours in between bringing up her children, she had under-school-age children for eleven years which produced 'a lot of pressure'. This pressure takes many forms besides lack of time. Diana Leonard gave a very simple example:

"The major problem was not sleeping for a considerable number of years, that just slows you down. With small children I don't think I had a solid night's sleep for five or six years."

There is also the perennial problem of divided loyalties between work and domestic commitments. This alone saps energy and creativity:

"There are always demands on your time, energies and concerns. When you're not fulfilling these duties, you feel guilty that these hapless children are being left while their mother goes out. . . ."

Guilt is still one of the biggest pressures which prevents women from taking time out to do what *they* want to do.

Divided loyalties and the guilt that goes with it is something that even women without families have to deal with. It is part and parcel of being unable to take yourself seriously as a writer, and if you are not convinced, no one else will be either; demands will be made on your time and energies in all sorts of directions precisely because you do *not* have a family and are consequently considered to have far more free time to spend at the disposal of other people. However much a woman detaches herself from the constraints of family or other relationships, there is still a strong undercurrent of feeling within her that, if it is required of her, and whether other people actively demand it or not, she must sacrifice time and emotional energy servicing other people — men or women   with whom she has no legal or biological connection.

THE INFLUENCE OF FEMINISM

Any woman writer today has to take some kind of position on the Women's Liberation Movement, whether positively or negatively. The

Movement has been in existence in Britain for ten years now, despite assertions from some — women as well as men — that it does not exist. Not all the women we interviewed saw feminism as the main motivating force behind what they were doing, but nearly all of them admitted that the WLM had had some influence on them.

Caryl: "It certainly had an effect on me, just the way it has affected everybody. Just more confidence in myself, questioning the way I was living and my relationship with my family. It's changed my writing in that it has become more consciously aware of these issues. At first when I started writing, I used to write more often about male characters because I wanted to show that I could, rather like the reasons I wrote plays instead of novels, I had to make something very independent and separate from me. . . . I never think 'I must have something feminist in this play', but feminist things are fairly conscious."

Despite this influence of feminism, she dosn't see it as her main reason for writing, since she had written plays and had them performed before feminism had become a political force:

"My encouragement as a writer came from a theatre doing a play, it came from the work done. But I was encouraged as a woman by the women's movement."

Other women do point to the WLM as having a direct influence not only on what they write, but in the way they write it. One of the most fundamental things that the WLM has insisted on is that because something is written down, it doesn't necessarily mean putting a 'line' or asserting some kind of Ultimate Truth.

Sheila: "The feeling that you are in a movement means that you believe that ideas are changing and are changed by what people are doing. There's no absolute feminist statement."

One of the major problems that women face in involving themselves in either political or academic life is that there is strong pressure to commit yourself to a particular line or theoretical position, and women have felt the need to resist this.

Sheila: "What has been very important to me is that I'm not writing something that has a claim to be some absolute finished thing. Part of the women thing is that you are writing something that other women are going to change. Therefore, all the terror which comes from competitive achievement, of writing an accomplished thing, which is an illusion which belongs to the male academic world, can be lifted by the fact that you can state: 'I'm not writing that kind of thing, if you want to write it, get on with it'."

A consequence of this is the reluctance of women who write and publish to be seen as in any way representative of the WLM, or any kind of spokeswoman for it. To perceive themselves as 'professionals' would in some way be adopting a label with certain assumptions and expectations attached to it which the WLM is trying to challenge. For example, the halo of authority which surrounds someone who has been (oh!) Published. Sheila described the battle she had in the early days of the WLM when she became a Name that the media could catch hold of:

"It was frightening at first that my name was known and not many other people's names. That was a terribly frightening situation because it was unknown, and I didn't know what I ought to do. Each time something came up like 'will you go on this programme' or something like that I had a decision to make about what I should do. It does not matter so much now because there's lots of women who've done things, but at that time it was scary because I didn't want to get isolated. The presence of people to whom I was just me was very important."

These two refusals are part of the growing belief that the printed word is not, and should not be, the province of an elite. You are no longer considered to be significant just because someone has decided to print or publish your opinions, nor indeed are the opinions themselves. Books are no longer oracles, but instruments.

Many women writing today see what they are doing not as some kind of superior creative giftedness, but as a more down-to-earth process of communication with other women. They do not write just to prove a point or to achieve fame, but more to raise questions and try to solve problems. This is the case with not only the more overtly 'political' writing of Sheila Rowbotham, but also for 'fiction' writers. Michele Roberts, when asked why she thought it was important to have her work published, said:

"Because I want to reach lots of women. . . . Just a need in me to speak to lots of women, have conversations, have my stuff read — I've got something to say. And I think therefore a thousand copies is better than five typewritten copies circulating amongst your friends."

COLLECTIVE WRITING

An important difference that the WLM has made to women writers has been the rethinking of ways of working. The traditional idea of the writer has been of an individual working in virtual isolation and finally producing either a masterpiece or a flop. The terror which this notion of the process can produce — which appears to depend on mystical inspirations and endless energy — has probably led to the sinking into oblivion of many promising writers. In the last few years, women have begun to construct support networks to help each other write. The writing is still done alone, but the groups of women meet regularly to give each other criticism and advice.

Some of these groups are content just to meet and show each other their work, and perhaps individuals will get work published, although not all women do want to publish. One group, however, has not only provided support for its members, but has also collectively published the results of three years' work together, under the title *Licking the Be Bed Clean*. We were unable to speak directly to the whole collective, but we spoke to Michele Roberts, and received letters from the other members about various aspects of collective working.

The group was set up in 1977 and holds two sorts of meetings. One sort is for support and criticism for anything women in the group happen to be writing, whether poem, novel, or short story. The meeting's time will be divided equally between the number of women present so that everyone has a chance to do what she wants, which is not always directly to do with the writing:

> "Whatever you want to do, you can do. You can read a poem, a short story, or you can just talk about a writing block you've got. Or if you want to, you can talk about your personal life, and everyone else gives you feedback and comment."

The other meetings are concerned with 'project work'. Originally concerned with producing the poems *Licking the Bed Clean*, they are now concentrating on producing a book which includes poems, short stories and pictures, commissioned by Sheba Feminist Publishers (see Chapter 4).

To publish their work collectively, they had to find the time and money to do it. The money came from a grant from the Greater London Arts Association, and each woman put in about £20 each to cover initial typesetting and printing costs. They needed a bank account for the money, and had to become a company (Teeth Imprints) to open a group account. They did most of the work themselves, except the typesetting and printing. The whole process took them eighteen months. They also took a hand in publicising it, sending review copies to magazines and newspapers. This got them reviews in *19*, *The Guardian*, *Time Out* and *Feminist Review*. They also did group readings to publicise the book at the National Poetry Centre, Centerprise Community Centre, and the Socialist Centre in North London. Finally, they also helped distribute it by taking it by van around to bookshops.

Their own efforts had a good effect on sales. They printed 1,000 copies initially, which sold out, then another thousand which have by now nearly sold out. For a supposedly minority-interest publication — since that is how publishers largely regard poetry — that's not bad going.

> Michele: "That's what convinced us that there is a market for feminist poetry, that you can tap through the underground and subculture. And actually your own distribution and printing is going to be much more successful than using a big publisher."

NOT ALL SISTERLY

This particular group does not *write* collectively, that is, they don't collaborate on a single piece of writing. The work done collectively is that of support and criticism and the project work involved in producing their collected work for publication. The writing of poems, stories, and so on is still done alone, it is a solitary process but no longer a lonely one. The existence of the group gave its members a feeling that they could and should spend more time on their own, doing their own writing and feeling less constrained by demands around them to do other things. This is seen as part of the process of taking themselves seriously as writers, of consciously adopting that identity for themselves. Related to this is the fact that nearly all the group have found the impetus to give up full-time employment in order to spend the major part of their time writing.

The group provides a situation where each woman gets the chance to share problems, which can be either the technical ones involved in a specific piece of work, or the emotional ones involved in writing. The trust which is built up over a number of years is a very important factor for all the women, and all have formed close friendships within the group.

It's not all sisterly, however. Some of the women admitted to feelings of jealousy and envy of other women's writing, and these feelings have been discussed in the group, which is an indicator of its strength. Alison Fell wrote:

"I have sometimes got into confusion and difficulty with the group idea . . . and also feel competitive and envious on occasion. If my own work feels awful to me, I can get very over-impressed by anyone else's writing, and feel very depressed and competitive. But the confusion that came up was the difficulty I have felt in showing my novel . . . And so I came very shamefaced to the group and tried to explain all this, and how unsisterly, uncollective and untrusting it all felt. It was a big relief to be reminded that the group was to be used for my needs, whatever they were, not as an internal pressure to be collective, sharing, etc."

Michelle Roberts was the first woman in the group to publish a novel:

"I'm a competitive person, I know I am. But you find that you've created a space where you can fight these things out, although it takes time. . . . Now that the others are all writing novels it's much easier to confess to them my envy and competition and not feel I'm going to damage them and stop them writing their novels. . . . I feel much closer to all the women in the group over the three years I've worked with them . . . that's partly because I've been able to admit to myself feelings of hostility which are not sisterly, but they are actually part of my feminism and I can now accept that. That's what's really good about being in a group, that you can do that, and have a good time."

For this kind of support group to function, however, there has to be a common basis apart from the fact that everyone in it is female. It is unlikely to work if there are power relationships cross-cutting within the group. Diana Leonard described the attempt made at the Institute of Education where she works to set up a women's group which could give much-needed support to the research students, and to the staff. The members included lecturers, research officers, research students and secretaries from the administration side:

"It wasn't a feminist group in curious ways. There were whole areas of our lives that we never talked about. For instance, our sexual relationships. We also didn't talk about our relative positions within the Institute. I always felt there was a good deal of tension between myself and one of the secretaries, but it was never discussed. I always ducked out of trying to describe it, I don't know why. I felt that because we all had to go on working with each other. . . ."

The tensions also existed between the staff and the students. The power relationships prevented some of the women from talking about the most important things in their lives:

"People found it quite difficult to be angry within that group, so it operated as a community group but not really as a women's group, which was why, I suppose, I never talked about my work there. For me to talk about my research in the group was to kind of display myself before them. Whereas for the research students it was to display their frailties in front of their supervisor. Or for the secretaries, it was a demonstration of the fact that they weren't actually producing the goods which count as goods in the academic community."

These conflicts made her decide not to continue going to the group, but she hopes that another group will be set up in the future where the research students and staff will have space to discuss their work. They will still have to confront the power relation.

IS THERE A FEMALE (AS OPPOSED TO FEMINIST) WRITING?

The question of whether there is a 'female' form of writing surfaces periodically. This is part of the debate about whether women can form their own culture which would be qualitatively different and distinct from the male-dominated 'patriarchal' culture which exists now. It is not just the question of the content, the subject-matter being different, but also whether language itself — grammatical form and syntax — can be altered to better express the female experience. There have been experiments made, mainly by French women (Monique Wittig and Helene Cixous for example), to create a different form of writing in this way, but so far, this aspect of the debate has not become a major issue in the British WLM.

An unlikely source of support for the view that there are forms of writing which can only be done by women comes from one of the editors at Mills & Boon, publishers of romantic fiction. She expressed the view that the type of escapist romance they publish *cannot* be written by men. The writer has to know what women want at a fantasy level, and men have no idea. There is a skill in writing in this way, however, and not all women can do it.

Perhaps of greater relevance with regard to the question of form is the choice of literary form in the sense of novel, play, poem, polemic, non-fiction, etc. Which of these forms is the best vehicle for the ideas a woman wants to put across? Caryl Churchill spoke about her decision to write plays in the context of wanting to produce an object definitely separate from herself, which she felt she could not do with a novel:

"I knew a lot of people who were writing novels and it seemed too easy almost. I wanted something which almost stood out from myself . . . I liked the discipline, the concentration of it."

In her view, there are relatively few women playwrights as compared to novelists. She saw this as being due to the fact that writing a novel is a more private activity, and for that reason it is easier for women to do it. Secondly, because women tend to write about subjective matters, a novel was a better vehicle for this purpose than a play, since a play is "not so wordy and has to have more events". Thus, women are less inclined to write plays "not because of their nature, but because of the kind of experience they get given".

On top of all this, there are the obvious problems women find in getting plays produced in a male-controlled medium. We discussed women playwrights with a literary agent, Anne McDermid, who emphasised the external causes rather than the internal ones:

"I think the main problem is the management. I know, for example, that the management of the National Theatre and the Royal Shakespeare Company, and certainly the management of the main West End theatres don't go near a fringe play by a woman when it's produced at the ICA or the Almost Free. They don't bother to go along, whereas they'd go along instantly to a David Hare or any of these male playwrights. Particularly of the left-wing, people who are talking of the appalling plight of the working man. Now I agree that it's a good thing that (this) be reviewed on the stage, but I also think that an enormous number of these plays are valueless compared to the staggering stuff which has been done by women about their own situation."

According to Anne, the main problem — apart from the blatant sexism — is the perennial one of who controls the purse-strings. In the theatre, like everywhere else, it is men; men who don't understand what women are trying to say and who aren't interested in finding out, hence they are not prepared to risk their money. In short, it's not that women don't write plays, but the struggle to get them staged is more difficult than getting a novel published.

WOMEN V. THE REST OF THE WORLD

Along with the question of which literary form they want to use, there is another issue for many women writers with respect to content. Women, perhaps as Caryl said, because of the experience they are given, tend to write about domestic or subjective matters more than men do. These subjects are traditionally seen as 'women's writing'. Several of the women we interviewed felt ambivalent about this.

Sheila: "(A woman in our writing group) who was very interested in women's fiction writing used to talk a lot about the way in which women like Jean Rhys write about a very typical inner personal world, because they live in these very domestic, intricate worlds. I always felt very ambiguous about that, because one's kind of fascinated and drawn by that world. At the same time, as a little girl, I wanted to get out of it, because I wanted to get into some kind of wider world also associated with men's world. I did not want to be confined by this sewing, ladies talk and things."

So the question for some women writing is that writing about the personal and domestic spheres is necessary to assert that the experience of women is worth discussing, but in so doing, they run the risk of being regarded as of only marginal interest because of that. The belief behind these statements is that eventually women must take their rightful place within culture and society on an equal level with men, rather than hive themselves off from men (although this might have to be an intermediate stage) to produce a separate culture of their own.

Diana Leonard had to confront this issue in relation to teaching Womens Studies as part of sociology. Women's problems and feminist politics provide the impetus for much of her work. Despite this, she never felt that to teach women's issues as a subject was the best way of promoting feminist ideas within academia. She chose a different method:

> "I've seen it as trying to operate within sociology rather than teaching women's studies. Although I've always done research on women and been particularly concerned by them. But I would always want to problematise masculinity, masculine practices within sociology, which I guess is one of my worries about women's studies and always will be."

To teach 'women' as a 'topic' is to concentrate on one sex alone and to ignore the fact that at least 50 per cent of 'the woman problem' is 'the man problem'. Rather than just accepting the position of it being just another subject area — to be taken up or not according to preference — Diana has begun to try and challenge the masculine bias of sociology, bringing out its inherent sexism:

> "I think that throughout I've managed to say some pretty outrageous things and dared them to ostracise me because of it. My strategy has been, for better or worse, to raise my head and say: if you shoot it off, it is a political act."

2
WOMEN IN THE PUBLISHING INDUSTRY

Publishing as we know it today did not emerge until the nineteenth century. Up until then, the printers operated as printer, publisher and seller combined. With increased literacy the growth in the demand for books meant that the printer/publisher had to produce more books and in greater numbers than before. This meant that the printer/publisher had far less time and resources to spend on the pre- and post-printing operations. These functions became the responsibility of the publisher alone, who also now takes on the financial risk of producing the books in the first place. The Women's Press gave a list of the different kinds of work they have to do as publishers, which included: advertising, publicity and promotion, direct sales, press enquiries, reading manuscripts, marketing, production, design, authors contracts, export sales, editorial, writing blurbs, catalogues, subsidiary and foreign rights sales. There are also functions related to storage and distribution.

THE GENTLEMAN'S PROFESSION

There is a basic contradiction in modern publishing which has not been solved yet and creates many problems: it is the discrepancy between the image that publishers still have of themselves as the 'Gentleman's Profession' and the change in the market which makes it impossible to be any such thing.

In the 1930s a number of houses were headed or established by men with strongly liberal views, from well-off families, who believed in the notion of a 'universal culture', one created by an elite of talent and genius who would tell us the 'ultimate truth' of our world. These men were typical of a certain class and Michael Lane, in his book, *Books and Publishers*, describes the archetype:

"We picture him as someone who is ultimately connected by ties of friendship or even kinship with the most distinguished members of our society's literary and intellectual elite; as someone who spends the greater part of his time in the company of men of letters. He is a writer himself or aspires to be one. He has a private income which he uses either directly to subsidise his business or indirectly so that he himself need not be governed in his decisions by such

crude considerations as making a living or profit and loss . . . His
only real interest is the world of books.''
So publishing was not a 'commercial' but a 'cultural' responsibility
which grew out of a certain class. However, the market forces and
the readership changed dramatically after the war.

THE SAGA OF CAPITALISM

Whereas before 1947 publishers had not needed to bother about
marketing, the growth of the market meant that after that date they
needed to invest fully to meet its demands and capital resources had to
be boosted. Many small houses whose commitment to literature was
stronger than their commercial sense found that sooner or later they
ran out of money, and they either went bankrupt or were absorbed
into a larger group. For example, Rupert Hart Davis and MacGibbon
Kee were both taken over by Granada, and are now called Hart Davis
MacGibbon, which is simply the hardback end of Granada paperbacks.
Moreover, an increasing number of these houses or groups of houses
are now wholly or partly owned by non-publishing companies. A good
example of both these trends is what happened to Cresset Press, a small
publishing house which used to publish many excellent authors, such
as Carson McCullers. It was bought by Barrie Rockcliffe, which in its
turn was absorbed by Barrie & Jenkins. They in turn were taken over
by Hutchinson, which is owned by London Weekend Television. It
could be worse — the American publishers Simon and Schuster are
owned by Gulf and Western Oil!

Thus, the typical middle-sized general publishing house which
prevailed until the 1970s is being replaced on the one hand by large
agglomerations of imprints, such as Associated Book Publishers, and,
on the other, by small, frequently specialised houses on the other —
the feminist Virago, Sheba and The Women's Press fall into this category.

The following table shows the number of titles printed in Britain
over the last three decades:

Year	New titles	Reprints or new edition	Total
1950	11,738	5,334	17,072
1960	18,794	4,989	23,783
1970	23,512	9,977	33,489
1978	29,530	9,236	38,766

Note that the number of new titles soared from 11,738 to 29,530
within 28 years, whereas reprints hardly doubled, thus books of quality
became unavailable in preference for rapidly replaced books which
could be freshly raved over and quickly forgotten.

These figures predate the upsurge of the crisis which has been grip-
ping publishing since the end of 1979. In real terms, publishing turnover in 1978 was 2½ times what it was in 1950; but an industry profit
of 1.5 per cent in the fourth quarter of 1979 became a loss of 9.6 per
cent in the third quarter of 1980. Meanwhile the number of titles
published in Britain continued to soar (to 48,158 in 1980).

Whether the present crisis is merely a hiccup in the profitability of publishing or marks a continuing slump in fortune, it is clear that one overall trend will continue — the sense of 'cultural' responsibility will come second to that of making profit. Publishing *must* now be primarily a viable business if it is to succeed according to capitalist standards, and the role of the accountants will become ever more important.

WOMEN IN THE GENTLEMAN'S PROFESSION

So where do women stand in this change? Very low. They have managed to insert themselves on the editorial side, but they have made few inroads into management and finances. They are still barred from these new areas of power and control. Even though women have invaded the base of the pyramid, publishing remains a male bastion, appropriately called a 'gentleman's profession', if not for the same reasons as before.

It could be argued that some women have 'made it'. Some of us are marketing directors, more are commissioning editors, but on the whole women are sparse where the power lies, i.e. on the board of directors. Looking at the 50 top British publishers we found that there are only 41 women out of 420 directors and major shareholders (individual, rather than other companies). The best sex ratios are at Andre Deutsch, with 5 women out of 13 directors, and at Michael Joseph, with 4 out of 11.

All our interviewees gave us examples of discrimination towards women, not only in training and promotion, two of the most predictable problem areas for women working in a male-dominated industry, but also in having to deal with seeing women as profitable 'products' as part of the new trend of publishing books with women as the subject-matter.

We interviewed three women for this chapter: Anne McDermid, a literary agent whose job is to get her authors the best deal possible with the publishers and all other media; Jay Dixon, who worked for Routledge & Kegan Paul and then Methuen for a long time, editing other people's work. She went freelance, which she has always intended doing, but the timing was brought about by the realisation that to become a commissioning editor she had a long fight on her hands, with no guarantee of success; Majo Xeridat who works for Macmillan as a designer. Her job is to help create and supervise the design of the book or magazine published. Although she likes her job she wants to leave, out of frustration, to pursue a more fulfilling activity: karate.

Women fit into a male-dominated industry, as expected, in its 'caring' aspects, in those departments where 'feminine' qualities are required. In publishing it is in editorial work and in publicity, as well as the normal place behind the typewriter. It is the base of the pyramid, without which there would be no summit; it has no glory and is badly paid:

"My firm is thought of as a women's firm because there are quite a lot of women working in all kinds of jobs; but the people in responsible positions are men. In my particular studio there are four designers, only one is a man. The other person is the art director: a man."

Women are attracted into publishing because it is a field where many women already work, and is obviously more interesting and stimulating than many other jobs open to women. But Anne McDermid explains how it can be seen as another profession where women fulfill their conventional nurturing role:

"The publishing profession has traditionally been a profession to which women have had access much more readily than others. From quite early on between the wars — which is rather earlier than other professions, women have been active in publishing, and I always thought it was partly because publishing is a *caring* profession; that is, it's a profession in which subtle psychological reaction is important. It depends upon understanding people's motives, being quiet and listening, caring for their emotional problems. This is why women have been allowed to play certain roles in publishing for many years."

This point is confirmed by Frederick Warburg's description (in an interview with Michael Lane) of one of his colleagues, Barley Alison, whom he greatly admired:

"She liked looking after her authors as a mother her children. She liked seeing, feeding, entertaining, supporting, encouraging them and rejoicing with them when they had success. She was, in my view, God's gift to a needy author struggling to gain a reputation without starving to death."

So, as long as women fulfill their 'natural' duties, it's alright for them to be in publishing. Along with the other caring professions it pays badly — even a commissioning editor would only earn between £6000 and £8000 per year. One wonders if it remains so because women are becoming more prevalent in such jobs, because, in spite of the probability of low job satisfaction and bad pay, women are still attracted by publishing. To help produce a good book could be a very creative and fulfilling task. But we say 'it could be' because too often for women it rarely becomes that.

Women are lured into publishing at a low level, such as secretary, with the hope, if they work hard enough, of eventually being promoted to the responsible jobs of commissioning editor and director, the elite which chooses which books the firm is going to publish. But for most women this remains a myth. All our three interviewees were adamant on that matter: don't start as a secretary or at a low level — the chances are that you will be stuck there for years.

Jay: "They've always said that the only way for a woman to get into publishing is to be a secretary. That works in some houses. In other houses you just get stuck as a secretary and they pay badly. It is bad throughout the whole spectrum, but especially at the secretary level, when you compare it with secretaries in other fields. They take into account that you do interesting work. It's true, it is interesting work, even as a secretary, but on the other hand there is the danger of getting stuck as one."

Anne: "I was told that in Britain you more frequently get onto a secretarial course after your degree and that seems to me to be death, for anybody who wants seriously to get on."

Majo: "When men start working they apply as graphic designers whereas women apply as assistants, and remain so."

We have been trained to think of ourselves so much as secretaries or the ones with artistic and literary inclinations, that we are not aware that there are other ways to get into publishing, e.g. technical courses like those at the London College of Printing.

WOMEN, THE UNIONS AND PUBLISHING

Even in this most genteel of industries, change is noticeable, and union strength is growing. The NUJ Book Branch gained 500 new members in 1980, whilst it lost 300 — but turnover is always considerable, and that year was one of very high redundancies. SOGAT/ATAES,. which organises in all the non-NUJ areas in book publishing, also reports a steady growth in membership, with the fastest increase in the clerical area, where there is the highest concentration of women. But despite the fact that the workers have (somewhat belatedly) started to get themselves organised, approximately 200 jobs were lost in the NUJ area in 1980, whereas in previous years about 50 were lost and 50 new ones created.

Many publishers are making staff redundant, only to rehire them later on a freelance basis to complete projects they had previously started. This trend has particular implications for women, as many of the jobs which are lost will be dumped on the homeworkers of the publishing trade — freelance women, who depend on casual work for the same reason as their less well-educated sisters turn out plastic toys and cheap dresses — they are tied by young children or elderly dependents. Some people, like Jay Dixon, choose to go freelance because of the flexibility it gives them, but it is this very quality of the freelance system which is of such benefit to the employer. There is no responsibility or liability for employees' security, yet there is a pool of diversified labour anxious for work. These are valuable commodities, especially in tight economic times.

Trying to safeguard the position of all their members, both freelance and tenured, is a severe problem for unions in the publishing industry at the moment. This struggle should be carefully monitored because women in publishing are generally perceived as having 'made it' in some sense in this society — more highly educated, earning above the average female wage, often with equal pay and fringe benefits, although we catalogue numerous instances where the reality fails to match the image. Nevertheless, it is a bad omen for women in the labour force in general if such women cannot hold their ground in the face of the recession and if more women than men are made redundant and forced to take lower paid jobs, lose maternity and other benefits.

EQUAL OPPORTUNITIES?

So, what are our chances of equality within the industry? Thin.

Training

Some publishing companies send their employees on day-release courses.

They send quite a few women but according to Majo, who successfully completed one, they tend to drop out after a year or so:

"I think they thought that what they were learning did not prove very useful for their jobs. Most of them were visual assistants, which is a very glamorous word for a boring job sticking on labels. They did not think they would become graphic designers anyway. The blokes were already assistant designers and the demands made on them were high, they were expecting to make a career out of it. Furthermore, the course is one day and one evening a week, from 9am to 7pm plus home-work for three years. It becomes a bit much if you have a full-time job and housework at home to do."

Even if quite a few women give up the course, the firm does not lose out. They still have one person who is working at what she was doing before, with the added advantage of being a bit more skilled, for the same salary. However, we are rarely sent on financial and management training. This essential knowledge is kept for men.

Another important aspect of training is the basic psychological encouragement, the informal chats with the boss and the incentive to improve if you work together well. There is no greater encouragement than letting your 'subordinates' hear the reasons why you make the decisions you make, treating them as intelligent colleagues. Too often, with women, bosses will keep their information and knowledge to themselves.:

"I'd come in and say 'I've got a historical novel'. He would just say no and wouldn't tell me why."

There is an information gap between the management and employees which is deliberately maintained, but men step across it much more easily than women. Jay gave us a good illustration of this:

"Two people joined at the same time, one girl in January as a secretary, one man in June as an assistant editor. The man at the top took a liking to him, as he was the only male companion he'd had for years. The assistant editor had very important authors shoved at him without any grounding in publishing at all. She, the girl, has never had this kind of help, and quite frankly she's bloody good, yet she is completely overlooked."

The opportunities in the publishing industry are biased towards men, and this lack of balance can make men *appear* better than women. Jay said:

"When a man has been promoted before a woman it's difficult to say that he is not better, when the chances are that since he gets more help, he may appear to be better. If a woman wants the help, people think: 'Oh, not another moaner!' They are not bothered with her."

Only by women having access to the right training and information will the situation of discrimination change.

Acceptance

Another consequence of women not being in key positions is that they are not taken seriously within the firm; it is much harder for a woman to gain acceptance and trust:

"If a man presents a design or an idea for acceptance to an editor or manager, they'll discuss it on the grounds of taste; but should I do the same things, I find myself questioned about everything in that particular design — like: 'Are you sure that putting the table in that place wouldn't be nicer in that place?' And then I say: 'No, I put it there for a particular reason.' So many years of experience don't seem to come into consideration."

Even if you are really good at your job, if you have to prove yourself constantly to other people, it undermines your self-confidence:

"On one of the jobs I've been doing, the printers refer constantly to my art director and not to me. They are constantly by-passing me, so they obviously cannot take it, that I am responsible for what I am doing — but if they *had* to come back to me as the responsible person, then yes, . . . from that you get a lot more confidence."

Even when women reach the position of selecting books, we still have to justify ourselves much harder, and justify our choices to the board; Jay:

"One woman I know who has been made a fully-fledged commissioning editor had an awful lot of difficulty getting material through, whereas the men (she's the only female on the board) had much less trouble. A lot of the men stand up in meetings and bang on the table and throw hysterics as far as I can see. She refuses to do that, and they're prejudiced towards her. On the other hand, a lot of what's published by her is well done, maybe because she always has to prove herself."

The discrimination we have discussed so far is fairly subtle, however we have come across quite a number of examples of more blatant discrimination. We will quote only one given by Majo:

"She was a woman assistant manager to a man. She was very good at her job and very experienced. When he left, logically she should have become manager. But she was considered to be slightly too young (26) for such a responsible position. They appointed someone else who'd been in the firm 6 months with hardly any training in that job, but he was a man. He was 28 years old!"

BUSINESS IS BUSINESS

Publishing is now a commercial venture and no longer a hobby. Still quite a few houses will publish a book for its value, knowing that they will make a loss on it. But the race for the bestseller, especially in paperback houses, is becoming fierce. One important outcome of that competition is the 'hype' when a huge amount of money is invested in one book which goes towards the rights for the book and above all to the advertising aimed at agents, publishers, booksellers and readers. Limited financial resources are increasingly concentrated on fewer products over a shorter space of time. Publishers become unwilling to keep books in print — even 'classics', if the turnover is not high or if they have not had much spent on advertising them recently. Bookshops become unwilling to stock books that have not had a large advertising budget, and therefore narrow their range of stock. The definition of what will sell, what is 'interesting', is more than ever determined by the profit motive, and the expectations of numbers to be sold spirals ever upwards.

The effect of all this on what is defined as 'minority interest' is clear: it doesn't get printed. This attitude of mind encroaches on all levels of publishing, so that often, even when a male academic publisher decides to take a 'risk' with a feminist book, he prints too few, so that its selling price is high, so then it doesn't sell very many copies and the gloomy predictions are fulfilled. And although feminists may be less reluctant to publish with academic mainstream publishers, as they have a more placid image than general publishers, the business practice of academic publishers is no better. Often authors are still denied significant editorial control, cannot discuss what goes on the cover (particularly important when fighting against sexism), and get ripped off financially.

THE AMERICAN SELL-OUT

The preference given by British publishers to American authors in some ways reflects the prevailing economic climate. Looking round bookshops it is immediately obvious that there is at least as much, if not more, American-originated feminist writing as there is British, and certainly more than the European countries put together. This is because the publishing industry in Britain is responding to the present recession by a massive contraction in commissioning original work, and to keep up their turnover of new books, they are buying a lot of titles from America. This means that quite frequently the only cost they incur before printing the book is an (admittedly substantial) author's advance to the American publisher to buy the work ready for printing — no editing costs, no proofreading, no indexing, no designing or typesetting, i.e. no work for employees, just income for the publishing houses and royalties to America.

Anne McDermid, the literary agent, explains how it affects her clients:

"The ultimate decision is the publisher's, and no matter how enthusiastic you are, if there is not a publisher around prepared to pay the money and actually buy that writer, you are still stuck. I'm dealing with two women whose writing is superb, much better than some of the American stuff, and I have not succeeded yet in getting them published. One of the reasons is that British publishers, when they want to publish for the 'women's market', invariably turn to the American market where it has already been tested."

Another reason for buying American is that it is in what seems to be the same language. But it takes no account of the different cultural systems between Britain and North America, and discards the cultural similarities we have with Europe.

Another important factor in this sell-out to the States is the dependency of British publishers upon foreign sales (mainly to America, but also to Australia and Canada). It means that they are less prepared to take a book which would sell only in this country. Why publishers have decided that a book about a Leeds housewife won't sell in Boston, whereas one about a Boston housewife will go like a bomb in Leeds is an unanswered enigma.

HOW TO MURDER A BOOK

Sexist book covers were one of the topics discussed at the conference of women booksellers, held in Manchester in February. We decided to campaign against this one, the paperback edition of *Fat is a Feminist Issue*, to be published in May.

The new cover is offensive and completely contradicts the content. As with most publishing contracts, the author has no power to veto the cover. It's particularly enraging that a feminist book should be sold in this way and that the word 'feminist' should be linked with such an image. It's being sold as a diet book: the picture is a sort of all-in-one-before-and-after-bait. What is the thinking behind such advertising? The cover repels women. Are the publishers just stupid or is the idea that some fella will connect with the image and buy the book for a woman?

We think the book is important to women and should be widely available at a low price, so to boycott the paperback would be self-defeating. Instead we are trying to raise the issue in women's magazines. In our bookshops we will display the cover and provide space for people to write their protest — which will be sent to the publishers. Anti-sexist bookmarks and stickers are available from Grassroots, 1, Newton St, Manchester — 24 stickers for 10p, 10 bookmarks for 3p (please enclose sae). And write to the publishers, Hamlyn, to add your voice in protest. ○

Sue Marshall, Alison Read
Hamlyn Group, Astronaut House, Hounslow Rd, Feltham, Middx

Fat is a feminist issue

In 1970 Susie Orbach joined a consciousness-raising group which concentrated on women's experiences with compulsive eating and self-image:

"At that time energy from the women's liberation movement sparked us all into rethinking many previously held assumptions. The creativity of the movement prepared a fertile soil in which feminist ideas, nurtured and developed in countless consciousness-raising groups, found new applications and usefulness. Compulsive eating was one such area."

"We had taken the formula of a women's group, and one by one we shared how we felt about our bodies, being attractive, food, eating, thinness, fatness and clothes. We knew enough to know that all our previous attempts at getting our bodies the right weight and shape had not worked. We wondered why we had wanted them so right, what was so powerful about looking a certain way that we had all tried and succeeded in losing weight dozens of times. We began asking new questions and coming up with new answers."

It is the accumulated experience of women who have suffered as compulsive eaters that has provided the answers to those questions and has led to the writing of this book.

Susie Orbach

A self help guide for compulsive eaters

Fat is a feminist issue

Susie Orbach

Fat is a feminist issue

Counter-cover

About this cover

This 'counter-cover' has been produced by a group of women who work as printers, booksellers and distributors.

We were angered to find that the publisher of *Fat is a feminist issue* had used a cover design which exploits women. It suggests: "Buy this book, and you too could look like this". The ideas that Susie Orbach expresses in her book completely contradict such an image; in fact she has found that some women are fat because they don't want to be seen as sex objects.

Publishers have total control over book presentation. Hamlyn went ahead with their cover design despite protests from the author, and they rejected the sub-title that she felt reflected the book.

So we decided: if they could produce their own cover, so can we. In doing so we have received support and involvement from Susie Orbach.

Join us in our protest by addressing your own complaints to the publisher: Hamlyn Paperbacks, Editorial Department, 103/105 Waterloo Road, London SE1 8UL.

The American sell-out is one response to the recession; another one is that more work is being printed, typeset or bound in Asia and the Far East, where costs are often lower, not just because of the relative strength of the pound, but because the workforce is not unionised and therefore employed under very bad conditions with very low pay; or else the printing is done in modern, capital-intensive factories which employ fewer people. In the case of some Eastern European countries, the State subsidises work from abroad (their own internal printing charges being very high), so that it can be much cheaper for British publishers to ship their work abroad to be printed, despite the cost incurred in doing so. Academic publishers are involved in these tactics as much as anybody, and thereby undermine the efforts of the British workforce in fighting for decent pay and conditions, including fighting against sex discrimination.

WOMEN AS SUBJECTS

The success of books like *Our Bodies Ourselves* and *Wedlocked Women* have shown that women's issues are 'a market'. We don't want to read only about romance as many publishers would like us to believe. Anne McDermid thinks that there is still a great resistance to publishing women's issues such as breast cancer or women's work:

"They are largely dismissed on the grounds that either the· subjects are too embarrassing and cannot be sold in bookshops because nobody would go and buy a book on that subject (in the case of breast cancer); or that they are of minority interest, meaning 60% of the population. It's still easier for publishers to think that women will buy a thriller for their husbands than that they might buy a book about childminders to help them actually go out and work."

Even if your book has been accepted for publication, there are still obstacles as Anne recalled about one of her authors, who wrote a book on rape. Everything went well and the publisher did quite a good job but:

"The publicity department was run by a man who had not the faintest idea how to publicise the book in the first place, or how to get it into the shops in the second place; he was apologetic for it from the very beginning, and he was staggered when the TV and radio programmes were after the author. He felt constantly embarrassed about it. Furthermore, I had many lunches with literary editors and people of that kind who, on learning that I had an author who had written a rape book would tell me the latest rape joke."

We should not be over-optimistic when we see more women's books on the market; Anne sees a real danger in this women-fashion in male-dominated publishing: they still retain the control. They can switch off whenever they want:

"I'm afraid we are not more in control of it than we were before, they've just decided that we are a market. They are not caring about what we read, it means that they want to make money out of what we read. If they decide to cut it off, that's it. We should be in control from beginning to end."

CAN IT CHANGE?

Some women think it can change, that a job in a publishing house can be really fulfilling if discrimination is eliminated. They, along with some more radical women, have set up a Women in Publishing Group. Anne described it:

"It will enable women who are doing perfectly ordinary jobs in publishing to at least feel that their lack of strength in their firm is not due to their own weakness, their own inability to fight. I'm sure that the only way to make a fundamental difference is for a lot more women to be in a position of power at the top."

Feminists in publishing must fight for an improvement in what goes between the covers of a book, and indeed *on* the cover. The struggle should be to publish books on new areas, in new forms, which avoid sexist stereotyping and the use of derogatory language about women which help us to form a new image of ourselves and our society. Women must become aware of the importance of the groups who have the power — those who hold the purse-strings, the board of directors — all male-dominated.

Some of us decided that there was nothing we could do in such a stronghold of male power, and we did not like their way of working, which involved a rigid division of labour and hierarchical power structure. They decided that the only way out was to set up their own publishing ventures, where they would have total control over working relationships and the product: these are the women's presses.

3
WOMEN'S PUBLISHERS

The advent of the feminist publishers in the mid-1970s has done more to promote awareness of and interest in women in the last five or six years than the whole of the male-dominated publishing industry has done in the last 50 or 60 years. To be (more than) fair to mainstream publishing, it has been responsible for the appearance of some of the modern feminist classical works. *A Room of One's Own*, first published in 1928 was republished by Penguin in 1945, and was reprinted several times in the 1960s and 1970s. *The Second Sex*, published in France in 1949 was published in England in 1953 by Jonathan Cape, and again in 1972 by Penguin. *The Feminine Mystique*, was published in America and in Britain in 1963 — the British publisher was Gollancz — and republished by Penguin in 1965. *The Female Eunuch* was published in Britain by McGibbon & Kee in 1970, and *Sexual Politics* in 1971 by Rupert Hart-Davis. Each of these has been reprinted since, in the case of *The Female Eunuch*, 15 times.

But at least part of the reason these books are labelled as 'classics' and made such an impact in Britain was because they were the only books of their kind at the time, there was little else to compare them with. The fact that you can reel off the list more or less on the fingers of one hand is dependent on this. It has only been with the rise of publishers run by women committed to promoting the interests of women both culturally and politically that we have seen the enormous output of books concerned with women — and this has affected mainstream publishing in its turn; having dipped only its toe in the water, it allowed the women's publishers to take the plunge.

There are at present five women's publishers in Britain, four of which (Virago, The Women's Press, Onlywomen and Sheba) are based in London, and one (Stramullion) in Scotland. There was one other combined publisher/distributor, Feminist Books, now defunct, based in Leeds, which published *Conditions of Illusion* and the very successful *Wedlocked Women* (1973). All the publishers see themselves to some degree as feminist, but how they interpret this differs widely. There is no doubt that without the existence and support of the WLM, they would not have got off the ground, but their relationships to the Movement are very different.

They all wanted to see women's culture available everywhere, and to change the accepted ways of working, hence they refused the traditional notion of employer/employee, and attempted to break hierarchical relationships. A women's press is not a temple of culture, it is a forum for discussion and creativity; women have and are producing much literary, theoretical and visual work, and it is the job of a women's press to give them the network of communication they need. To quote Onlywomen Press:

"In order to create a Women's Liberation Movement reality, we need discussion and the development of political analysis unhindered by patriarchal values. We need a means of establishing our own culture."

Feminist publishing, more than any other aspect of the book production process, seems to epitomise most clearly the problems and choices which face feminists confronted with a society which is both patriarchal and capitalistic, and the differences between the five publishers are a reflection of the different choices they have made in order to go about the business of disseminating feminist ideas.

To state the issue in its most general form: what are feminist priorities, and how does one go about achieving them? For the feminist publishers more specifically, the problems are: to what audience are they appealing? how many books and how often do they want to publish? what sort of material do they want to publish? Is it better to create a climate in which feminist ideas are made more generally acceptable, and so produce a more commercially acceptable product? Or is it more to the point to publish things which are new in concept or approach because they are valuable for the WLM while not necessarily being saleable in a wider market? Or do you try to strike some sort of balance?

It is a fact which is disagreeable to many feminists that to produce any commodity, including books, in large quantities, it is necessary to become immersed in the aforementioned patriarchal and capitalistic world of business. Setting up a structure to produce thousands of books necessarily involves raising capital and, unless you happen to know a socialist or feminist millionaire, that capital will have to be raised somehow, either by gifts, loans, or advance sales. To maintain financial solvency, interest on the loans must be paid and the loan itself repaid. The Women's Press currently pays c. £6,000 per annum in interest payments. Virago has similar kinds of commitments. Some feminists argue that the overriding need to stay solvent means that a blander, more commercial product is produced, and this dilutes the feminist message.

At least two of the other women's publishers decided that they did not want their publishing programme to be affected by large interest repayments. Onlywomen and Sheba made the decision that they were as much interested in *how* the books and other material were produced as they were in the product itself. Their priorities are, in principle at least, to change their working relationships to what they see as a more feminist way of working, as well as to produce feminist books. Because of this, they refused the avenue of borrowing capital to set themselves up, and raised the money to finance their publishing programmes in other ways. Onlywomen functions as both a printer and publisher, and

finances its publishing partly by printing. It also has received grants,
loans and gifts. Sheba started its own mail-order catalogue to get money
in advance through subscriptions, and also relies on loans, grants and
gifts.

The price both these pay is in producing fewer books on a more
obviously precarious financial basis, but they do, again in principle,
retain a greater measure of independence about the books they will
publish, in the sense that they are more prepared to risk publishing
unusual or original kinds of work. For instance, Sheba is keen to break
away from the printed word and produce more mixed media and visual
work; Onlywomen is now producing a series of pamphlets on health.
The other price they pay is literally in pay; they cannot afford to pay
good wages, if they pay them at all, and so rely to a large extent on
voluntary labour, although this is not something they want to continue
doing indefinitely. Virago and the Women's Press pay reasonably well.

VIRAGO

"We feel strongly about publishing books which express the ideas of
the women's movement in a way which makes them accessible to the
widest possible audience of both sexes, and we feel strongly about
publishing books which reflect many different views within the
feminist movement. We also want to publish books which illuminate
women's history and women's lives and experience in such a way
that the value of this culture can be understood by everybody."
Originally set up in 1973 with a capital of £1,500, Virago became an
associate company of Quartet Books which provided them with much
financial support, and then went independent in 1976. It is a limited
company with 3 directors, 7 shareholders and an advisory board of
about 32 women. At present there are 4 other staff besides the directors, and 1 part-timer. They pay themselves equal salaries, apart from
the trainee, and operate a fairly definite division of labour, where each
director has separate, overall responsibility for the areas of finance,
production and editorial, although there is a certain amount of overlap
between them in the day-to-day working.

Virago are quite candid about working in a hierarchical way, but say
that because they are a small company that in practice everyone becomes involved in the discussions and decision-making:

"If you are a small company, usually everyone is in the room discussing everything at the same time. Our hierarchy is less rigid than a
collective. If anyone wants to do something she can do it, unless it
costs money, in which case she has to talk about it with the rest of,
us."

Like all the women's presses, Virago faces the problem of producing
print-runs of 5—10,000, which means that they are more expensive
than mass produced paperbacks (which have print-runs of tens of
thousands). One of the ways Virago is dealing with this problem is to
get some of its typesetting done by a company based half in Scotland,
half in Hong Kong, which is cheaper than getting it done entirely in
Britain; they justify this choice, which many would criticise, saying
that their main target is to reach as many people as possible:

"The reason for this is because British setting is now so expensive that we had to choose between making our books available at prices people could afford or not publishing the books. We feel very strongly that our books should be priced as reasonably as possible and look as good as our competitors."

Up until now, Virago's prices have been in the £2.50 — £3.50 range on average; this is slightly more expensive than The Women's Press books, which averaged between £2.00 — £3.00 for the same period.

What they publish

Virago's publications are divided up into Fiction, Virago Modern Classics, General and Handbooks. Within the VMC series, there is a small section entitled 'The New Man' which consists of books about women written by men, and includes books such as Gissing's *The Odd Women* and Meredith's *Diana of the Crossways*. The fiction section, consisting mainly of original novels written recently by women, is not a very large part of their output, but has included *Benefits* by Zoe Fairbairns and *Tea and Tranquillisers: The Diary of a Happy Housewife*, by Diane Harpwood. The largest single section of their publications is the Virago Modern Classics series, of which they have so far published 53, with 13 forthcoming. These are entirely fiction reprints, and include titles such as *Two Serious Ladies* by Jane Bowles and *My Brilliant Career* by Miles Franklin when it became a highly acclaimed film. Virago have been criticised for this concentration on reprints at the expense of newer work; however the importance given to reprints is partly a reflection of their aim to establish the existence of women's culture more firmly in the public mind, and partly a financial consideration, since not only do reprints usually cost less than publishing a book for the first time, they also sell fairly well.

The General (non-fiction) section includes a wide range of material: autobiography, biography, sexuality, gardening, science, health, history, literary criticism and education. Some of these are original works, such as Monique Wittig's *Lesbian Peoples* and Sheila MacLeod's *The Art of Starvation: Anorexia Observed*, while a few are reprints, such as Ivy Pinchbeck's *Women Workers and the Industrial Revolution*. The Handbooks include subjects of general ocial welfare, such as the problems of disabled women and how to organise home births.

At the outset, they did intend to give much more support to new women writers:

"When we did our first leaflet, we said the reason we set up was to highlight all aspects of women's lives . . . We were set up to be here to help and advise women who wanted to get published and work closely with them on their manuscript. Lots of women we first published were not experienced writers, and an enormous amount of work had to go in to get their manuscripts into shape, more than if we were a commercial publisher.

Because of constraints of time and money, original works were for a time a smaller part of their publishing programme, two thirds of their list being reprints. They are now increasing their output of original works, twelve in 1981 and twenty in 1982, as part of their overall

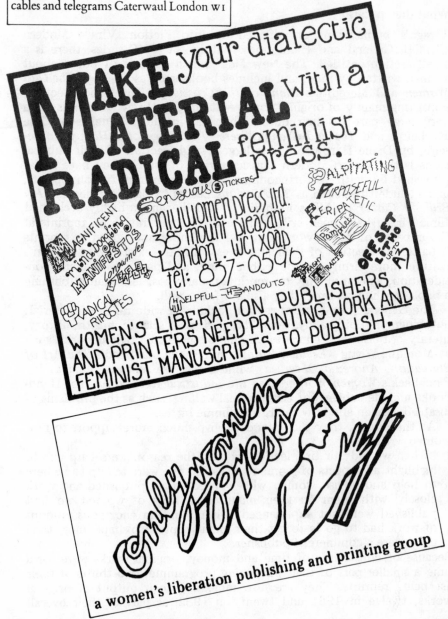

expansion. They have been publishing about 40 books a year, which they intend to increase to 50 in 1981.

ONLYWOMEN PRESS

"A group was established in 1974 in the common understanding and determination to publish and print feminist books, pamphlets and posters, etc., with all production carried out entirely by women. Being part of the Women's Liberation Movement has meant to us not only recognising our oppression, but resolving to overthrow it and, therefore, to withdraw support for any of its systems that we could by establishing our own."

Onlywomen operate as printer and publisher, and see the two activities as mutually supportive. But for the convenience of our chapters, we discuss only their publishing activity here. The historical background is provided in Chapter 7, and their comments on the importance of publishing pamphlets are in Chapter 4.

Because of their commitment to controlling as many aspects of the production process as they can, Onlywomen necessarily do not publish as many books as a normal publisher would do, but what they do publish they see as vitally important to the WLM, and to extending women's culture. They are a collective of four women, with a support group of four other women who write as well as giving them assistance and moral support:

"In commercial publishing the process is incredibly split up from place to place. Here we are trying to pull the whole thing into a more integrated activity altogether. It's out of a feeling that we need control over our lives."

To help integrate the process, Onlywomen Press operate a task-sharing system, where all the women learn how to do all the different aspects of the processes of printing and publishing.

What they publish

Partly because they have little money, and partly out of political choice, Onlywomen so far have published mainly pamphlets, although they have also published a book of current British feminist poetry *One Foot on the Mountain*, and a novel by one of the collective called *Cactus*; they intend publishing another novel (*Brainchild* by Eve Croft— in the spring of 1981. The point about publishing pamphlets, from the practical point of view, is that they are able to both print and publish them themselves. Books they can publish, but cannot print and bind, since they do not have the money or machinery to do so. They have started a new series of political theory pamphlets, of which *Hard Words* and *Women and Honour* are the first. Because they can be produced quickly, these are seen as a contribution to the discussion of what is happening in feminism now. They have done one on health, *Down There* (about self-examination) and a second is planned. They are also compiling an anthology of radical feminist theoretical essays, and have produced a series of postcards and some posters.

As for the future, they do not see themselves getting bigger all the time:

"We will publish the books we feel are necessary and important to the Women's Movement. We do not see ourselves tied to a linear concept of expansion where one makes 'targets' of so many books per year . . . We exist as a press as a form of commitment to women's liberation, and thus operate to put out the books we need — a varying number."

As part of their commitment to the WLM, they assist in the promotion of their publications in particular ways. For example, they organised several poetry readings in London when *One Foot* was published, and hope to do this again with future publications:

"We are quite committed to making what we do an act of participation within the Women's Movement instead of turning out products like hot dogs."

This concern is reflected in their relationships with their authors. A very important consideration for a writer is the extent to which she will have control over her work once it is in the publisher's hands. Only-women Press is particularly concerned to respect their authors in this, and have drawn up a contract which reflects this intention:

"We use [the Writer's Guild] contract with some additions of our own, like stating at the beginning that we are a Women's Liberation group. On the list of terrible sabotage which nobody is responsible for — like fire and flood — we've also got patriarchal sabotage, which they thought was quite funny; it's also been quite real, it happened to us."

THE WOMEN'S PRESS

"We aim to publish work which reflects the goals of the Women's Liberation Movement, which is accessible in language and price, which looks good enough to compliment both the writer and the reader. We see our work as publishers as part of a circle of women talking, writing, reading, engaging in many activities, passing ideas to each other, some of which . . . take shape in book form."

Founded in 1977, The Women's Press began to publish in 1978. It has financial backing from the Namara Group of companies but despite this, The Women's Press say that they have complete autonomy to publish what they want, and that no associate company in the group influences their editorial policy in any way. Quartet Books, one of the associate companies, sells their books in the UK and also helps with production, but they do all the other work of selling and publicity themselves. There are now three full-time staff and two part-timers. At the beginning there was Stephanie Dowrick with Sybil Grundberg working part-time, and they had a group of ten women from whom they got advice and support. As the Press became established, this group ceased to function. At the present time, Stephanie takes the responsibility for the major decisions, because she is the most experienced member of the Press staff, although all the workers have a say. In the future, they plan to divide up the work and responsibility more equitably.

The workers at the Press all have different responsibilities in the different aspects of the production process, and there is also a differential in salaries based on experience and responsibility. One of the

part-time workers has a young baby which she brings into work since the Press feels it is important not to exclude women who have family responsibilities.

They have fewer people working at the Press than they would like because they do not take on volunteers on principle because it is too reminiscent of the traditional view of women volunteering their labour.

Like Virago, The Women's Press does not use women printers, since at the present time, they have neither the facilities nor the skills to produce books on a large scale. But The Women's Press does sometimes use Red Lion Setters for their material, and would be very reluctant to send their work abroad.

What they publish

The Women's Press publishes a wide range of both fiction and non-fiction books, they also reprint neglected books by women, but concentrate more on newer material. They are also developing more visual books (on art history), posters and postcards, and generally trying to promote women's art work. They always use women illustrators for their books.

At present, they publish 15 books each year, three of which are reprints. Over half of them so far are fiction titles (25 fiction, 17 non-fiction), and eight have already gone into a second printing. Their fastest selling books include several modern writers such as Marge Piercy and Michele Roberts. They do not publish books by men. Several of their books have been produced by groups of women who contributed pieces. These include *Hard Feelings*, *Why Children?* and *Learning to Lose*, and the Press intends to continue this kind of collaboration where possible.

All their books are printed in paperback, and they are now trying out hardcover editions to sell to libraries in order to support the paperbacks. Like Virago, they face the problem of producing print-runs of 6-7,000 in the face of rising printing and paper costs, while trying to keep their prices as much in line as possible with mass market paperback prices:

"Our only solution to this problem is to be able to sell more copies of each book, and sell them faster, as we are borrowing our production money at 21 per cent currently."

To increase turnover, and make books more widely and cheaply available, they have launched the Women's Press Book Club, which enables readers to buy at much reduced cost, both their own books and those of other publishers.

SHEBA FEMINIST PUBLISHERS

"Sheba is a feminist publishing co-operative run by a group of women from within the Women's Liberation Movement. We were brought together by a shared need: to see both more and a greater variety of publications committed to feminism in bookshops and libraries everywhere."

Sheba was formed in January 1980 by a group of seven feminists. They set up a business co-operative, and are all equally responsible for running the company, there is no hierarchy of control. They are non-profit-making in the sense that any money they do make immediately goes back into the business, but three collective members now do five days waged labour in the office each week. All other labour is voluntary and shared among the collective — each woman contributes at least half a day unwaged labour per week.

Each member of the collective has been or is involved in some aspect of the book or magazine trade, so they all have different skills to contribute. They see the task of demystifying the different tasks in book production as very important, and endeavour to teach each other the different skills, such as paste-up, design, and so on. They made a definite decision at the start that they did not want to set the business up along conventional lines:

"We talked and decided that we could do basically two things: we could either set ourselves a time limit and get money together and all that, or we could just literally plunge in.

It's a belief that women *can* do it. We've been told for so long that we can't, it means capital and so on."

The money to start was raised by donations, loans (paid back at six per cent interest) and through mail-order by which Sheba offers its books at a reduced rate to anyone who orders them in advance. All this is necessarily a rather precarious situation, but they feel it is worth it to preserve a large measure of independence:

"I think it's a very feminist way to do it. The cheques had 'good luck' written on the back. They seem to feel they're helping us start. It's not a straight demand for money."

But can this way of doing it withstand the financial pressures they are facing in the longer term? The collective seem fairly confident that it can, and this came out in their discussion of promoting visual work:

"I think a lot of the commercial publishers shy away from posters because they are not commercially viable, and if you're out to make a profit you're going to do it in the fastest way you can. Although we have to break even and make a bit to keep going, we're not interested in that above all else. That's why we think we can do it."

What they publish

Sheba is keen to break away from the publisher's traditional reliance on the printed word, and are trying to produce books and pamphlets, calendars and postcards which stress the visual aspect of information much more. For instance, they use illustrations from their books as both a publicity point and a selling point; they print illustrations from their books and sell them as postcards, saying which book they're from. Of their first list of five books nearly all use illustrations as an integral and important part of the books.

They also want to produce short, accessible, theoretical texts, and children's books, which none of the other feminist publishers are doing at the moment. Their first book, *Sourcream*, was cartoons by several feminist cartoonists, and is selling well, partly through being sold by W H Smith — which they are very pleased about, since it means it will reach a wider audience.

Sheba
Feminist
Publishers

183 Swaton Road, London E3

a Scottish-based feminist publishing collective

Besides producing books which are reasonably priced and popular, they also want to put out books which are contributions to the Women's Liberation Movement, such as *Women and Russia*, which is a "complete translation of the first issue of a new Russian feminist magazine, published in Leningrad last December and immediately suppressed by the KGB."

STRAMULLION

Stramullion (an old Scots word meaning 'strong woman') is a Scottish-based publishing collective which was set up in 1980, and produced its first book, called *Hens in the Hay*, in November 1980. This is an anthology of poetry written over the previous 18 months by some members of the collective, and illustrated with drawings by others.

They are a collective of seven women committed to skill-sharing, and the money for this first project was raised by personal loans and a grant from the Scottish Arts Council. There is a support network of women involved in printing, publishing and bookselling.

Their first priority is towards new work, either from Scottish women or relevant to Scottish women's experience.

There are one or two other feminist publishers groups who produce material that is not just printed words. For example, in Britain we have See Red Poster collective who intend to give positive images of women in a visual way. In the States there is an even more innovative form of feminist publishing. Black Box is '. . . the first literary magazine to be published in cassette format.' It offers a return to the tradition of oral poetry — where the distinctions between songs, chants, theatre and poetry are broken down.

CHOOSING BETWEEN A FEMINIST AND A MAINSTREAM PUBLISHER

With the increasing commercial success of feminist publishing ventures, it is not as easy as it once was to make a definite distinction between them as a group and the rest of the publishing world; they are not all just 'alternative' groups. Although some of them might accept that label more readily than others, all of them see what they are doing as qualitatively different from mainstream publishing. Virago said:

"What we discovered when we were at Quartet was that they did not understand — and they were in no way subnormal — that what we do is special. It would be fair to say that many of the books that Quartet would not take on, because they thought they were not viable, became very successful. They did not see the audience."

From the point of view of a woman who wants to get a book published, especially if it is on a subject concerning women which has not been written about before, she probably stands a better chance of getting it published by a women's publishing company. Some women make a political decision that even though they might be commercially successful, they want to put their name, prestige and income-generation into a press which will help other women who don't carry the same weight in the commercial world of publishing, e.g. Marge Piercy. But for other feminist writers the political dilemma is more difficult. To be published by a large commercial company almost certainly means watering down the content of the books, and having decisions about style of presentation, publicity and promotion and so on decided for them. The main advantage is that their books will, potentially, be available to a wider audience, since larger companies have greater resources.

This is perhaps one of the main problems for feminist publishers since it is obviously not the case that the books they produce don't sell, but the scale on which they are produced is so small, despite the fact that they can be reprinted, and their promotional budget and sales force is limited. For instance, Onlywomen Press' poetry anthology, despite it being their first book, and having an extremely low publicity budget, sold out the first printing in only five months. This is a particularly notable achievement, as poetry books are the most difficult to sell.

In view of the fact that 40 per cent of The Women's Press books are sold abroad, they maintain good links with several feminist publishers on the continent. Sara, a Dutch feminist publisher, distributes *Gyn/Ecology* in Holland, for example, and The Women's Pess stresses the importance of sharing information and knowledge to support one another:

"The most tremendous support is the feeling that they are there, they listen, give advice, and above all face the same contradictions between selling, buying and their politics and so on."

But the attitude within the Women's Liberation Movement is still ambivalent:

"There's still quite a lot of unease about us doing what we do, and seeming to do it well. This is often disguised with a kind of moralism instead of being dealt with very directly . . . about what it means for some women to have a certain power, and other women not to have that power."

This is an issue which is rarely mentioned in all the rejoicing when women set up in business for themselves, or attain skills which have traditionally been denied to women, and it is a general question for all feminists, not just those in the women's publishing companies.

4
SELF-PUBLISHING AND THE IMPORTANCE OF PAMPHLETS

Publishing and printing books is a highly specialised and capital-intensive operation. Few women as yet possess the skills and even fewer possess the money to enable them to do this; as yet none of the women printers we know of have the skills or capacity to print books. Women's self-published writings are thus largely published in forms that require fewer skills and less money — in the form of magazines, booklets and pamphlets.

The idea of self-publishing has been growing rapidly in the Women's Liberation Movement over the last few years; it is recognised by women that while some women's writing will be published by commercial publishers there are certain things that publishers will not touch, partly because they are not mass-appeal items, and partly because their importance is not recognised.

The reasons for 'doing it yourself' do not only stem from the problems of getting a book or pamphlet through the commercial channels; there are three other reasons. Firstly, many women want to be more involved in the process of producing their own work. Secondly, to publish yourself means that no one else can control what goes into the book or pamphlet, or how it is designed and put together. Thirdly, the ideas that women want to put forward are often of an exploratory and tentative nature, less suited for this reason to the book form, which implies something more permanent. Adrienne Rich's *Women and Honor: Notes on Lying* is an example of this.

One of the most important ways, historically speaking, that alternative ideas have been spread — since the introduction of printing — has been through the pamphlet. From the fifteenth to the early nineteenth centuries, Britain had a flourishing tradition of political pamphleteering, despite the attempts of the State to suppress it. Pamphlets had obvious advantages — they were cheaper to produce and easy to read — although most of them were still too expensive for the poorer people; as an early historian of pamphlet literature put it:

> The Poor find their account in Stall-keeping, and in hawking them: the Rich find in them their shortest way to the Secrets of Church and State. (Quoted in L. Shepherd, *The History of Street Literature*, p. 25. David & Charles, 1973.)

During this period, they were produced by printers without the medium of a publisher, since publishers as a separate entity did not appear until the nineteenth century. Women were a part of this tradition. The seventeenth-century records of the Stationers' Company show that there were at least 60 women printers in Britain, some of whom brushed with the law over what they printed.

The nineteenth century saw the development of the rotary press, a much more expensive but more efficient piece of equipment, and the days of the small, independent printer were numbered. Those with money took over the trade, and were less willing to publish material that could be construed as seditious or libellous; controversy was absorbed into the newly founded newspapers, becoming distinctly watered-down in the process. Needless to say, women were not part of the new controlling power.

The impact of pamphlets rapidly decreased with the increasing influence of these new mass-communication forms. In the twentieth century the advent of television, radio and the mass-produced paperback virtually wiped out the pamphlet for a time as having any significance. But it has received fresh impetus as a form of communication since the late 1960s when new political ideas were in ferment, and since the rising cost of paper made larger productions more difficult.

Today's pamphlet, especially those produced in the Women's Liberation Movement are concerned not only with theoretical and political questions of feminism and socialism, but there is also a vast range concerned with issues of health, law, poetry, third-world women, education, history, childcare, etc.

WHY PAMPHLETS ARE IMPORTANT

Lilian Mohin of Onlywomen Press told us why she thought pamphlets are important:

> "Partly because of the size, they seem less formidable to read and carry. But also I think from the point of view of the way women are writing which, because of the kind of life many of us lead, and the way we think of ourselves as writers, ideas come out in very small bits . . . they do not fit into the existent, traditional format."

It's also important from the point of view of documenting the history of the Women's Liberation Movement:

> "Women's Liberation history is being destroyed by not taking ourselves seriously and not seeing ourselves as part of history. It's impor-that we not only make a record of what we've done, but disseminate these things as we go along."

An obvious advantage of pamphlets is that they are cheaper and easier to produce, and also to distribute, although some bookshops are reluctant to stock them because they are difficult to display and take up a lot of space. The cheapness of a pamphlet is of great importance when the subject-matter is how to claim social security benefits for instance, where the women who will read it necessarily have very little money. All the women who published pamphlets made cheapness one of their main objectives.

We interviewed two groups of women who had published pamphlets of very different kinds. We spoke to one of the women from the now defunct Women's Rights Group in Manchester, who published a series of pamphlets on legal rights in housing, social security and marital breakdown in conjunction with the local law centre. One gay woman from this group went on to publish a book with a group of lesbians and gay men called *Law and Sexuality*, and also, along with other women from Grassroots, helped Fanny Tribble publish her now well-known book of cartoons called *Heavy Periods*. The other group was at the WRRC in London, which publishes a series of pamphlets which are items of research done by women about women, largely during the course of university work, which otherwise would be left unread on the library shelves.

HOW THE MANCHESTER WOMEN DID IT

The Manchester women had the support of the local law centre in running a series of evening courses on various aspects of women's rights — housing, social security, marital breakdown, etc. The women running the courses set up as a Women's Rights Group in 1975 when the Sex Discrimination Act and other legislation affecting women had been passed. All had been involved in legal or advice work of some kind.

Having built up a good deal of information in these areas from the shared experience of women who attended the centre, they decided that it would be useful for other women to know about it. They had the choice of either running the courses again or publishing, and decided to publish. They were anxious that the information should be accessible to as wide an audience as possible, so they made sure it was written in simple language and that the price of the publication was kept to a minimum.

The women didn't allow themselves to be put off by lack of money; they did the first pamphlet and then borrowed money from the law centre for the print bill. This was the start of a programme of publishing material on women's rights by the centre, but at the time the women found it difficult to persuade the law centre to foot the bill:

"It was difficult to make them understand that we could sell the pamphlets and they would get their money back. To them it looked as though we were spending a few hundred pounds all at once and they couldn't afford it."

The women were not paid for their work on the pamphlets. To write them they took notes from the course meetings and took them away to write them up. They would then have meetings to discuss what each person had done; then they typed it up. A lot of the typing was done by one of the women at the law centre in work time. Quite a lot of thought had to go into how they wanted it to look before they typed it, since they weren't going to use a typesetter:

"We typed it in the actual size it was going to be reproduced so we had to know what form we were going to do it in. We decided to do a small size pamphlet because these are easier to handle, being more like a book, less like a newspaper. Then we got letraset and did the headings. The illustrations we found by going through old magazines and cutting them out . . .   . The thing we had most problem with was getting the pages in the correct sequence — because of going to the printer."

The printer was Mosside Press (see Chapter 7), who gave them advice on layout, paste-up and other technical details. The first print-run was 500 copies which sold out fairly rapidly and sales covered the printing costs. They did later editions which were better in terms of presentation — they did them with stiff covers instead of soft ones for instance — which cost slightly more, but were still within the reach of the women who needed them. The higher price was not only to pay for a better product, but also to pay for postage when sending them out.

The pamphlets were sold through the law centre, Grass Roots Bookshop in Manchester, and through mail-order. They were publicised through articles in *Woman's Own* and the *Manchester Evening News*. They were taken to women's events and occasionally they would be given away.

HOW THE WOMEN'S RESEARCH AND RESOURCES CENTRE DID IT

The series of pamphlets produced by the WRRC is also organised on a voluntary basis, although unlike the Manchester group, the women at the WRRC don't do all the work themselves; they pay to have the typing and paste-up done because they don't have the time. The group varies in number and are mainly women who have academic or publishing jobs. Originally there were 7 or 8 people involved but at the time of writing there are only three who are active and they want to recruit more.

The group is in practice more or less autonomous from the rest of the WRRC. They produce about three pamphlets a year at present. Diana Leonard told us why they had thought it better to produce pamphlets rather than a journal for getting the ideas across:

"It gives us much more flexibility in the length of thing we produce. Rightly or wrongly, journals tend to go for a fairly standard length . . . whereas we can go from 30 pages to 130 pages if we wanted."

There were benefits for the readers also:

"They can just buy the thing they want, otherwise they either have to buy a journal with things in it that they're not particularly keen on, or they go away and photocopy it. It also stays in print longer and is more easily available."

They produce two kinds of pamphlets; one sort is a shortened version of a Master's degree dissertation and the other is a collection of articles on a common theme, sometimes by different authors, which gives a specialised collection in one booklet.

How do they choose which things to publish? The collective chooses from material sent in to them, and from their own knowledge of who is doing what. They like to get original research material rather than research done on secondary sources, and they don't commission stuff.

Their organisation is now more sophisticated than it was at first. They used to pay a university print department to print the pamphlets which also bound them in basic, cheap grey cardboard. Then they'd

have to take the pamphlets off in a van or car and hawk them round to
the bookshops, having to go back later to pick up the money. It was all
very time-consuming and they lost quite a lot of money. Now, they get
the manuscript typeset and the paste-up is done by the printer — both
women-only companies. Like the Manchester women, they have gone
for a better presentation in the later editions and more unified format.
Distribution has improved since they now use the ubiquitous PDC.

PRICING

Diana Leonard was very informative about the problem of how the
WRRC charged for the pamphlets. They operate a 150 per cent mark
up. If the pamphlet costs them 40p they will sell it for £1.00. The
extra money pays for review and complimentary copies which go for
free; a certain number go to copyright libraries and to the national
libraries in England, Scotland and Ireland. Further, the WRRC has an
exchange agreement with other organisations in other countries, sending their publications abroad and receiving others in exchange. Then
there are the distribution and printing costs; PDC take 50 per cent of
the price of every item they distribute, and the printers and typesetters
require advances for work done so that *they* can pay *their* costs. Cash-
flow is a big problem:

> "We've got problems because so much of our money is locked up in
> the stock we've already got. You give PDC the stuff with an invoice
> and they pay you after three months. There was a stage when that
> was OK because we didn't have to pay the printer. Nowadays prin-
> ters want at least the money for the paper in advance, so as soon as
> you book in it you have to pay them £150 in advance, and they
> want to be paid as soon as they've finished."

Thus, in order to publish the material in the way they want they have
had to put up the price; the reader pays for a better product which is
more efficiently produced and distributed.

ACCESSIBILITY

Both the Manchester group and the WRRC collective are concerned
that the material in the pamphlets is easily available to as many women
as possible. This is seen not only in terms of cost and outlets for selling,
but also in terms of the way in which the ideas are put over. For the
Manchester women, the task was that of rendering bureaucratic and
legal jargon into plain English. For the WRRC the question of language
hasn't been so easy to resolve. The style and presentation of Master's
degree theses isn't usually accessible to the ordinary reader. They have
developed a system of checks to try and get round this. Firstly, they get
the author to go through the work taking out the academic bits, i.e.
those parts which prove that you have surveyed the field of literature
and are able to say where your research fits into it. Secondly, someone
who knows little about the area goes through it and marks all the words
she doesn't understand, and as far as possible these are translated into
easier terms. How far it is possible to translate this 'difficult language'
into 'ordinary laguage' is an interminable argument. It is undeniable
that academic writers frequently use a style of argument that can often

be put into more straightforward language; but it can also be argued that new or complicated ideas remain difficult to comprehend even when they can be described in familiar *terms*, just because the *concepts* are unfamiliar; in short, it isn't simply a question of using jargon where familiar terms would do equally well.

PUBLISHING A BOOK

While it is more difficult and expensive to self-publish a book than a pamphlet, it's not impossible. The Manchester *Law and Sexuality* project started out in a similar way to the pamphlets, only this time an outside group interested in gay rights got in touch with the law centre. It began as another pamphlet, but grew into a book. Again, there were problems getting money from the law centre which finally would only put up part of the cost. To get the rest of the money they did an appeal in the gay movement and raised £1,000 in gifts towards keeping the cost of the book low enough for the people who needed it to buy it. Grass Roots Books put in the rest of the money.

The process of producing it was at first very similar to that of the pamphlets. The group allocated each person a chapter, they then went away and researched it, wrote it, then had group meetings to discuss what had been done. Again the work was voluntary — including the typing, checking, taking it to the typesetter, and reading the proofs.

"We just did the best we could, asking people who'd done it before what to do next, working through it logically as to what was to happen."

Even at those parts of the process they couldn't do themselves they kept a close eye on what was happening; they designed the cover themselves by looking at other books and deciding what they wanted. They talked to the cartoonists to find out what cartoons were possible. They went to the printers and worked with them on laying out the pages in order to have more control over the design:

"Lesley, who was a printer, was there while they did it to make sure they didn't get the cartoons in the wrong place or chapters split wrong, and she was there to see what it looked like at the end of the laying out stage."

The printer was the Russell Press in Nottingham, a workers' co-op which they felt they could trust. They didn't use an 'alternative' printer because it was too big a job, and they didn't want to entrust it to a commercial publisher because they didn't want to water down the politics in it. The binding was done by a binder that worked with the Russell Press. One of the difficulties about getting it printed in Manchester was that there wasn't an alternative press which had good direct contact with a binder they knew.

Part of the reason why they felt they could undertake so large a project was the fact that some of them were working at Grass Roots Books, and this made things easier in several ways:

"We're dealing with books every day . . . I don't think we'd have done it ourselves on that scale if we hadn't had that space and continuity, if there'd been just six of us who'd worked in odd jobs here and there. We're not a group anymore, we weren't once the

book had finished. Who'd have taken the responsibility for making
sure the books were stored adequately and got sent out for the next
two years?''
They printed 5,000 copies including 200 hardbacks for libraries and
the book covered its printing costs within 18 months.

HEAVY PERIODS

Fanny Tribble is a cartoonist who was well known in the Manchester
area but not elsewhere — until this book of her cartoons came out. On
the strength of the fact that Grass Roots had been partly responsible
for *Law and Sexuality*, she approached them to see whether they would
help her to publish some of her cartoons. The women at Grass Roots
were interested but didn't have the money. They went ahead anyway,
however. Fanny got a collection of cartoons together — she chose
them herself, there was no editorial control — and Grass Roots said
they would publish them so long as they didn't have to find the money.
Fanny got a loan from Northwest Arts, and scraped the rest together
herself. So it was basically Fanny self-publishing, but using Grass Roots'
name and the experience of the women there; Moss Side Press and
New Manchester Review also gave advice.

They discussed as a group with Fanny what it should look like, the
format and the price. They used a commercial printer this time, one
that did a lot of work for the student movement in Manchester, because
it could do the wider format they wanted. They had 2,000 copies
printed and sold them all in the month before Christmas. They have
since printed another 4,000 which are selling well.

The publicity was basically review copies, press releases and an
information sheet saying what it was and where it was available. Storage
and distribution was again through Grass Roots. Fanny was to be paid
for the work she'd put into it, and sales from the first print run gave
her a lump sum, while the second was managed on a royalty basis.

DO IT YOURSELF

All the women we spoke to had learned a lot from the experience of
publishing things themselves; they felt they'd gained a further resource
for the WLM generally:
  "I think it's important for the women's movement that there are
  women around who know how to do every stage of getting something out. It's important that there are women's presses and women's
  publishers. And people who know how to do self-publishing as well
  as publish for you."
Not only did the women gain confidence and skills by going ahead and
doing it, but they also made available information and ideas which
otherwise would not have been widely available. It is also another step
away from the notion that a thing is only worth publishing if you can
persuade someone else to publish it for you; the idea of 'vanity publishing' has prevented many people from even entertaining the idea
that they should publish their own work — whether literary or otherwise.

5
ILLUSTRATORS: THE CASE OF THE VIRTUALLY INVISIBLE VISUALS

The expansion of lithographic printing techniques in the 1960s meant that illustrations could be incorporated in books and magazines far more easily and flexibly than before; because of this, many more books these days carry illustrations — photographs, drawings, etc. In the past, what an illustrator produced became, in practice, the property of the publisher, but in recent years, due to increased use and importance of illustrations, illustrators have been insisting on retaining the copyright of their own material. This change indicates how little importance used to be given to book illustration — but how far have things changed?

The status given to the activity of 'writing' has meant that the visual aspects of information have been down-graded. An author might be paid a pittance in relation to the time and effort they put into the work, but at least that effort is (usually) recognised. For an illustrator this isn't necessarily the case. The work done on a cartoon or picture is far less obvious than that done on producing an article or book. This may be because a book takes up more space, takes longer to assimilate and is apparently a more complex object, whereas an illustration is confined to a limited space and is almost immediately assimilated by the viewer. Whatever the reasons, illustrators can meet problems in getting what they do taken seriously. Jo Nesbitt wrote:

"Most problems stem from the way visuals are assessed — as 'inferior' to the printed word, not as complementary to it. So illustrations are used as space fillers or extras. Because of this, people are less willing to take seriously the question of visuals, how they use them, and how to treat the people who produce them. One misapprehension seems to be that cartoonists operate from the wrist down, requiring no effort of mind; it's not regarded as work, so that payment seems superfluous."

THE STORY THE PICTURE DOESN'T TELL

The process of producing an illustration or cartoon can be a very complex and time-consuming one. The preparation for a single drawing may take weeks or even months. The artist may have to read and understand articles, chapters or whole books — often on subjects they have little knowledge of — in order to produce relevant illustrations. 'Roughs' have to be produced and discussed with the author or publisher, and this can involve a lot of running around — more time and expense.

The production of the drawing itself is also more complicated than is apparent from the final result. Jo Nesbitt, for example, might draw several different versions of an idea and discard them before presenting one she and her client are happy with. That drawing itself may only have taken twenty minutes to do, but getting to that point might have taken several days or more of drawing. Other artists may spend a week on the one drawing which they present as the finished product.

COUGHING UP GETS THEM DOWN

All this work which goes into the preparation is invisible, it is not apparent on the printed page and is therefore not acknowledged and frequently not paid for. This is the case in both general, commercial publishing, and in radical publishing. As so often happens, money is the indicator of the value placed on work, but getting a reasonable amount of money for a job can be a struggle since publishers seem reluctant to approach the question:

"It used to surprise me how much of the 'gentility' of the straight publishing world carries over into alternative publishing. But if you're on the receiving end it makes little difference whether the publisher is skirting around the difficult topic of money because it's so vulgar or because it's all capitalist crap. I suspect that the motives behind each position are not very different."

For feminist illustrators the question of payment for work is a difficult one. On the one hand there is the question of doing work which you agree with politically, and you know the people concerned don't have much, if any money; on the other hand there is a certain amount of resentment when people expect a woman to produce work, unpaid, as a matter of course:

"Obviously there are many groups who genuinely have little money to spare — most of us have supported such groups for years by working for them for nothing or for a token fee; when they are groups that we feel some particular commitment to we will continue to do this. But something which all groups should consider, when they have decided to produce any kind of publication, is that since they have obviously decided to meet all the costs of production, why exclude the producers of their visuals from this process? They are as much a part of the production process as typesetters, printers and distributors . . . . If someone wants to produce something at their own expense, fine, but they really should think twice before inviting someone else to become another unpaid worker. It is particularly annoying for women to be expected by left and feminist organisations to slip into their traditional role of unpaid worker."

Jo Nesbitt said she had only met one person who straightforwardly said 'How do you feel about doing some unpaid feminist work?' without apology or coercion. She felt that this was the best way of dealing with the issue, since it left her free to say yes or no without feeling guilty.

The prevalent attitude towards visuals is illustrated in other ways, too. Work may be changed without permission — things are added or deleted from drawings. Permission to use material is sometimes only sought at the last minute when the work is already at the printers. The assumption is that so long as what is being produced is broadly left-wing or feminist that the artist couldn't possibly have any political or theoretical objection to 'contributing'. The idea that the artist might want to read and assess for herself what she's unwittingly contributed to is almost seen as an insult by those who want to use her work.

6
TYPESETTING

Typesetting is one of the first mechanical processes which, added up together, will eventually give a book. When a manuscript is ready it is 'subbed', that is, it is edited for spelling and grammar mistakes and inconsistencies of style and 'marked up' to be sent to the typesetter. Marking up consists of setting out the specifications which indicate to the typesetter exactly what the designer wants. The specification shows the typeface required, the leading (space between lines), column width, style for subheadings, paragraphs, footnotes, bibliography, index and any other detailed requirements of typographical style. The mark-up on the manuscript should show at a glance when to insert **bold** or *italic* type.

Understanding these instructions is one of the skills involved in typesetting, as the terminology used is that which applied originally to the hot metal process of printing. With the advent of the modern keyboard, mechanical/photosettingg techniques, typographical effects can be obtained which were impossible with old-style composing. The new technology has played a vital part in opening up the industry to women. The IBM Selectric (manual) composer made it feasible for the first time for some women (admittedly, only a very few) to set up in business at home. However, the NGA took a long time to recognise keyboard techniques at all, and when they finally did they only signed up those with office premises — you couldn't join the union if you worked at home. Guess who that discriminates against? Recently, however, the union has relaxed somewhat on this point, though how many women were forced out of business because they couldn't get enough work to cover machine-rental, only IBM would know!

The two most popular methods of setting copy for offset litho printing are IBM composing and photosetting. In the former, changes of face and size are done manually and for justified setting (straight right-hand margin) it is necessary to programme in textual requirements and replay the text for finished setting — a time-consuming process. In photosetting the copy is transmitted onto a disc a bit like a record. The disc is then put through a phototypesetter producing a cassette sensitive to light which is then developed, fixed and rinsed in a photo-processor. The final product in both cases is a length of white paper on which the copy is set, ready for paste-up, or as is, from which the printer can make a negative and plate to print from.

There are two 'women only' typesetters: Red Lion and Dark Moon. They both set up to make a living and not specifically to service women's or other causes but they are very different in their approach to work. Red Lion Setters include ten women who discuss business during a communal lunch and has its quarters in a carpeted, spacious office full of brand-new machines that they are buying.

Dark Moon comprises three women and corresponds much more to what one would expect of a small women-only typesetters, working in a small office with only two machines — one of which is mechanical and owned by the business and one electronic machine which is hired on a monthly basis. They live off the business but their salaries are not high.

WHY ONLY WOMEN

Red Lion in a way just happens to be an only women company and they quite enjoy this although they think sometimes of getting men in, because to them working with women is only a phase to gain confidence. Once you've reached it, why not men?

"It was just that we were a couple of women friends who grew to about three or four women and we really found that it was a tremendous relaxing and interesting situation. We found that we were able to talk about a lot of things that we hadn't been able to talk about before. We also found that we could be much more ourselves and that certain women were not as threatened.

Things are constantly changing. I don't envisage that there will be a man at Red Lion Setters in the foreseeable future, unless the union imposes it on us. But against that one has got to say that it is a process and not an exclusion for all time. We've got a lot of men who've entered our lives as customers and that sort of thing. We are operating out of a new confidence in being able to deal with them and they are not threatening any more. It depends on the men and the women. It's like when we employ women, it depends on the women."

Dark Moon do not agree with this view, and are far more radical:

"There is no question of a man ever working at Dark Moon. There is also no question of a woman being an employee on a permanent basis. We want everyone who works here to be an equal partner — ideally with three of us sharing two machines, working three days a week each, which is what we're trying at the moment. So we don't have 'vacancies' and the union can't impose men on us.

Dark Moon is for us a space women have made for women. It's not a question of not having the 'confidence' to work with men — it would be going backwards. Dealing with men who come into the office as customers has been quite straightforward. On two occasions we have refused a customer because of sexist behaviour, and from time to time we refuse copy which is sexist. Knowing we have that choice makes a world of difference to dealing with those men."

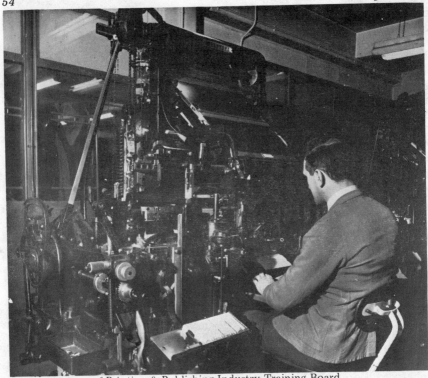

Photo courtesy of Printing & Publishing Industry Training Board

Big machine, big man.
The old style 'hot metal' process of typesetting is still widely used, especially in the
newspaper industry.
Small machine . . ..

Photo courtesy of Printing & Publishing Industry Training Board

ON BEING SELF EMPLOYED

Both typesetters admit to gaining a lot of confidence from being self-employed and in charge of their own work. A woman from Dark Moon explained:

"I never thought I'd find relating to men 'difficult'. I had stopped relating to men as a positive choice, to share my energies with women. However, after three years on the poverty line of Social Security there seemed to be no choice — it would have been crazy not to take the opportunity to set up in business. This way I had the possibility of earning a reasonable living with a skill I already had and enjoyed using without compromising myself with either men or employers.

During these three years, I have also gone 'temping' several times in straight jobs — each time I have been amazed at how much I usually take for granted, the freedom to come and go, to refuse work. Although this freedom can sometimes be an illusion. The work has to be done, often under considerable pressure, and half of the money we earn has to cover overheads. Nevertheless, I do recognise the extent to which I exercise control over my working life."

MACHINERY — A POLITICAL CHOICE

During our interview Dark Moon raised the very important question of the relationship between the machine and its operator, and the type of work a particular process generates. Red Lion Setters have several brand new electronic machines which allow them to take on big jobs and be terribly efficient, but at the cost of having to cut down the setting of what they really care about; they helped launch *m/f* magazine by giving them an extremely low quote but are unable to accept all the jobs they'd like to because the people just don't have the money.

"When you say working viably and commercially, you say working within the system and the system is very tough. We cannot accept all we'd like to."

The choice of machine is important not only for the type of customer it brings but for personal job satisfaction too, as Dark Moon explained:

"While I can see that the quality of work produced is greatly inferior on the manual composer, it remains the case that of all the different types of composing technology I've seen, I'm least alienated by the manual. The electronic requires a greater degree of concentration. With the manual I can just cut off and think my thoughts. With photosetting technology there is either eyestrain and headaches from working with VDUs (Visual Display Units) or what appears to be the total alienation of 'feeding in' on a 'blind' keyboard. Added to this, working with the chemicals required for the fixing process in photosetting is an extra health hazard."

UNIONS — WHERE TO FIGHT

Both Dark Moon and Red Lion Setters are in the union (NGA) because they need it for work, printers would not take a job without the union sticker. They are not active within it, although one of the women at Dark Moon has considered joining the Gay Workers in Print group.

She has felt that over the years the union has almost exclusively represented the interests of the craftworker, who is usually white and male. This has led the union to policies which exclude other groups, one of the more blatant of which is that mentioned earlier of confining recognition to those chapels with office premises. This is a more obvious example of the way in which unions, under cover of opposing the imposition of new technology for all sorts of 'sound' political reasons, in fact preserve their territory as white and male, but in the longer run find they have less and less territory left to preserve. Because she feels that gay politics could challenge this status quo in the union establishment, she might be prepared to put her energy into a gay group.

"I feel very dubious about it, but I do feel that I woudn't be forced to defend my lesbianism in such a group. I don't see the possibility of a lesbians-in-print group getting off the ground, not just because of the difficulties in setting up such a network but also because, like in my own case, I can understand lesbians not seeing union politics as a priority area for their political activity."

WOMEN: A SURE WAY FOR DEVALUATION

One of the most puzzling experiences of Red Lion is their difficulties in recruiting women typesetters. The only skill required is a good typing speed and a good level of English, the pay is very attractive (£7,000 per annum) and the atmosphere fairly easy-going. They run a permanent ad in *Time Out* to no avail. The job does not attract feminists because typing is a traditionally feminine skill and they are wary of it.

"It's a very strange job because it's a very odd combination of skills. The sort of person who is prepared to sit all day in front of a machine, but also has got to have a good standard of English and also bear the responsibility. Normally you are talking about a middle-class person who has a certain level of education. Middle-class feminists anyway, certainly don't expect to do typing as a job, and if they do, they expect to be some sort of P.A. or some title which gives them a certain position, some training in something. The tradition of people who failed their eleven-plus many years ago now, was to do commercial subjects like typing. So you had all your so-called failures doing it and there's a certain stigma attached to typing."

Many more women who have the skill are mystified by the word 'typesetting' and by an only-women collective:

"Most of the women who come here for interviews are terribly nervous and frightened of what is going to be demanded of them, because they don't have any idea of what typesetting is. And of course, a lot of women like working for men. They feel protected, there's some position."

If a job is done by women it is automatically devalued in society's view, as the bitter experience of Red Lion has shown:

"All the women here have had problems either from their husbands because they are working with women's groups, or more commonly, from their parents. One woman we had here, her mother said: you have an Oxford degree and you are cutting up pieces of paper all day. And she was a director of the company, but a director of a women's company — you know it's like saying nothing."

FOOD FOR THOUGHT

Dark Moon made us aware of another problem — the principle of a sliding payment scale. While they agree with having one, they can't help feeling frustrated when they compare their income with that of some people in radical groups which bring them work:

"I don't think it always works (the sliding scale) in that I find myself typesetting at a cheap rate for a group politically right on and poor. But some people in that group are on really good jobs earning 3 times as much as I earn and I find myself sticking a bit at that one. I'm just subsidising them. People can be guilt-tripped at that point quite easily."

The typesetters seem to share quite a few common points with their sisters the illustrators. Like them, they are low-status and often badly treated. It seems unfair, since the production of a good book involves not only a good writer, a good printer and a good publisher, but also an original illustrator and a very competent typesetter.

7
PRINTING

There are at least five print shops in Britain run entirely by women, of which we interviewed three — Onlywomen and Women in Print in London, and Mossside Press in Manchester.

Mossside Press started in the late 1960s as a mixed underground press with equipment donated by the Student Christian Movement. Luchia describes how, in about 1973, all the men left, and a couple of women who were around made it into a women's press:

"We did that very consciously, because at that time, just about 7 maybe 8 years ago, a lot of the women around were very political and very angry and wanted to have something of our own. Women's centres, battered wives refuges and everything were all springing up at that time. I thought it would be really good if we had our own media because I saw women come into the press and be treated differently from men who were getting their stuff published and printed. At first it was really hard because a lot of the left-wing men couldn't accept that it was an all-women's press, and some people were frightened that it was going to be all these radical lesbians, because we were known to be radical lesbians. They thought it was a real separatist thing at the time, which was a dirty word. We had to say: no, it's not like that. That all seems to have filtered away now."

Soon after women in Manchester took over Mossside Community Press, women in London started meeting to discuss starting a women's press there. A large number of women with divergent interests were involved, so that there was a split along very crude ideological lines, about whether to print things that had some sort of men's involvement, or whether only to print women's work. It was the original Women in Print group that opted to print men's stuff, as long as it was anti-sexist, and initially they had a man working with them, who knew how to print. Like all the groups, Women in Print has had a gradual change over of workers. Obviously the politics and the practice of the groups have varied according to the personnel, but all within a shared commitment to feminism and to collective working.

ACQUIRING PRINTING SKILLS

The women involved in Onlywomen Press acquired their printing skills by getting grants to go to art college for 2 years. While they were there they produced pamphlets, posters and a calendar on other people's equipment. After training it was not immediately possible to get premises and equipment because, as is usual with feminist enterprises, there was no money. Also energy had been diminished because of splits within the group. They eventually got a small press together, did quite a lot of printing, published *One Foot on the Mountain*, an anthology of British feminist poetry 1969-1979, and got some gifts. This helped them buy a Rotaprint machine which meant they had to move, as they could not get it into their basement — which was a great blessing! The new premises and new machine have meant a great improvement in their working conditions and to the work they can do.

Many women may be attracted to the idea of working in printing, yet feel unable to cope with the machinery and the necessary technical expertise. Although the first women at Onlywomen Press learnt their skills at college, subsequent workers there, and the women at Mossside and Women in Print have learnt as they went along, sharing knowledge between them. Luchia at Mossside is in the union, and can therefore train other women officially, if they serve a two-year apprenticeship with her. It is difficult for an untrained woman to get a job in printing, while the vicious circle is perpetuated by the unwillingness of conventional craft unions to take on women apprentices. It is possible to bluff your way in, but a lot of women don't have that confidence.

All the women printers acknowledge these difficulties and are determined to overcome them. At Women in Print, all the women were apprehensive about the machinery to start with. As one said:

"It's quite hard overcoming the mystique that surrounds the machine. It's like the first time you change a fuse on a plug, you feel a real sense of achievement, even though it's a miniscule everyday thing in the minds of so many men. I really find it exhilirating to discover that what's happening is quite mechanical and quite straightforward. A goes onto B and locks onto C; and that's really lovely. It makes you feel really strong and good and able to tackle anything — we hope."

Another woman said she was very intimidated by the actual printing machine:

"I learned all the other processes first and they were very simple and easy in a way, as you could see what you were doing. But working on the actual printing machine, I just had a sort of block against it. I've only just started running it this week, and I'm astounded . . . you *can* see why it's happening. If a disaster happens, it doesn't mean that you collapse hysterically and get carried out, you can do something about it. I overcame my panic by having some other people around who knew more and could tell me, and also as I was doing it, I realised that everything is explicable and that if you just bend your brain to it you can usually work out what's wrong."

WHY A WOMEN ONLY PRESS?

Working in a women-only group is to challenge male control over a whole sphere of activity — printing in this instance — and just by

INTERIOR OF MISS FAITHFULL'S PRINTING OFFICE, ESTABLISHED FOR THE EMPLOYMENT OF WOMEN.

Women printers have been around for a long time.

existing, they spread the idea that women can achieve things. Women give each other more responsibility sooner, as they don't assume you are stupid if you don't know things. So women feel less frightened of making mistakes or admitting what they don't know.

For all the women's presses, working in the way they do is part of their practice as feminists. They want to understand and have control over all elements of production; they believe that women must have access to the machinery which will allow us to produce material that men will not print; and working in a women's group allows feminist solidarity to be developed.

Most of the women initially involved with Onlywomen were writers. "We felt strongly that it was impossible to be writers in the way that patriarchal society demanded . . . We did not want anyone else to have control over the rest of the processes. So that means being involved in all the shit work, all the technical work, becoming involved in the craft. That meant each of us learning how to print and so on. We wanted to do it out of our feminist principles, really getting hold of that craft, making it ours, which also means doing it well. We don't think it's bourgeois to print well, even beautifully. We only thought later that it would be a good thing for women to be doing a job that is traditionally defined as male."

Predictably, getting caught up in the mechanical necessities of the press has left the workers with practically no time for writing. But as they take on more women, they hope this will change. They try to integrate all parts of the process and have a wider editorial and publishing group made up of full-time printers plus women who are not employed by the press, which provides a valuable source of advice and support.

Women in Print emphasise the positive advantages of working with other women:

"There's no competition, there's no hierarchy. We put a lot of time into discussing how we work together, we all feel very aware of how we relate to each other — not in an alienated work sense, but in such a way that if anyone's feeling pissed off or freaked out, we can discuss it. And it's nice to be with just women. A lot of conversations come up spontaneously about sexist things. I think our conversations would be much different if there were men around, even if the men were into non-sexist politics."

Whenever men become involved in a work situation, however peripherally, the power relationships of sexism, either subtle or intentional, quickly show themselves:

"When the mechanic comes along, I feel completely helpless, I feel I haven't got any power. You feel that you have to leave him to get on with it. Usually we try and watch exactly what he's doing, so that if it happens again we could do it.

So many things arise when men explain things to you, there's so many barriers and assumptions . . . . There's this feeling of oppression all the time, even if what he is explaining is perfectly straightforward and practical. And the man must want to teach you too, otherwise you can ask a question and he will half explain, leaving the freedom of the press belongs to those who control the press.

WOMEN IN PRINT   poster by see red

out something really basic because he doesn't think that you're really going to understand it. In those circumstances, you don't have any control over whether you're getting the right information."

One of the presses has been particularly fortunate to find a male mechanic who does some repair work for them free, not because he is politically involved, but because he is interested in what they are doing and recognises that they care for their machines. But often, interaction with men has been difficult for all the groups, as men seem threatened by the fact that the workers are all women, and by the content of their work. When Mossside first became an all-women shop, some of the left-wing papers they were printing at that time pulled out and went to commercial presses, because they had no confidence in the women's ability. One of the things that annoyed student papers especially was the fact that Mossside would not print some of the magazines that had sexist cartoons in, feeling that would be prostituting themselves.

As examples of why we need control of our own work, we were told what happened to the printed sheets for the Matriarchy Study Group's pamphlet, *Menstrual Taboos*, when it was sent to the binders. A member of the group went to see why it had taken so long to do the job and she found it had been put in the rubbish bin, because the binders disapproved of it. They were able to rescue it. Onlywomen Press had to deal with getting *One Foot on the Mountain* produced, as they could not print it themselves because of its size. The first printers they went to were very polite and friendly until they got the manuscript. Suddenly, they became very rude and did a terrible job on the photographs, used the wrong paper, and refused to keep to time schedules, so Onlywomen was forced to start again elsewhere.

In answer to: Why a women's only press? Luchia, of Mossside replied:

"Well I suppose I'd ask why not? Why the hell not? Men have dominated printing and the print world since the year dot, like they've taken over and dominated everything else. Around the time women took over the press we were all talking about equality. We thought: we don't want to jump in on the whole equality thing and be like men, we wanted something of our own . . . like collectives, an alternative . . . at least we're trying."

WHY COLLECTIVES?

All three presses see working as a collective as an important part of their political practice. This means that there is no hierarchy, decisions are taken equally by all workers, and tasks are shared, though how this is achieved varies between groups. At Mossside, a lot of discussion goes into work-sharing, because without it, they feel that each of the three present workers would go her own way:

"Luchia has been here for years so she tends to do all the printing, Gwen tends to do all the plate-making, and Angela tends to do a lot of the books.We've been pulling ourselves up a lot on it, saying we have to stop this kind of role playing, we're very conscious of it all the time. But task-sharing is not just an abstract political ideal, there are good practical reasons for it: I don't think anyone should have sole responsibility, say for all the accounts, which are a real head-ache. If only one person can print, and that person leaves, where does that leave you?

If somebody only does one thing all the time she might not understand the problems of my part of the process. If something comes out of the darkroom that's not quite right, instead of com-plaining, she will realise that there's something wrong with the developer, she can help solve it. It also prevents anyone having special power over the others."

Women in Print has gone to great lengths to avoid anyone being able to wield that sort of power. When we talked to them, most members of the collective were quite new and were learning the skills together. Rotation of work had only been instituted for about a month at that time, and they felt it was working quite well. There are three areas that they divide between them. These are plates, co-ordinating, and printing, so two people are on each of those, changing around if it becomes necessary. They try and guage work for the week, bearing in mind any particularly urgent job. but aim to be flexible, so that if someone spent two days one week making negatives and got fed up, she could move on. They recognise the possibility of somebody being unwilling to share her skills, but so far it hasn't happened. At that early stage of learning they decided on one occasion to give up a job rather than be put under pressure, as this would have meant being forced not to learn together. Obviously sharing skills equally would not be a problem once they were all more experienced.

In a collective that is working well, the mechanisms can be left to individual choice:

"There are tasks that are nice and tasks that are boring and mundane, and we all seem to do our fair share of them. It just works. Sorting's really boring, but sometimes I quite like that because it leaves you free to be talking to other people. You're able to have a nice long think which you don't usually have time for."

But unfortunately, relationships can go sour, as happened at Moss-side Press at the end of 1978. The resultant political and personal arguments reverberated through the whole women's movement in Manchester for months. The conflict is relevant for everybody concern-ed with the politics of collective working. This dispute, like most others, could be interpreted as a clash of personalities, but everybody involved agreed that there were important political lessons to be learnt, and as in all feminist politics, the personal is not divorced from the political.

At Mosside, the dispute arose because some of the collective tried to sack one of their members, and she felt. that, not having any other means of arbitration, she would call on the women's movement to decide the justice of her case. Important questions were raised:

"At what point are you answerable to the women's movement as a women's press; secondly what is the women's movement; and thirdly, what *is* a women's press? People asked us what we printed and who we printed for. We couldn't say we only printed for women. I think a lot of people hadn't quite realised that, and we got a lot

of flack for doing stuff for mixed groups, whereas the six of us had
never pretended to only do women's stuff."

The controversy did not arise over political differences or over what
should be printed, however, a sharp split was evident over the related
issues of workers' control and accountability. One side felt they wanted
to run a workers' co-op under workers' control, and that any group of
people from outside telling you how you should be working, no matter
how politically sympathetic, would be going against the principle of
co-operative self-management. It all depends on whether you see such
an organisation as a co-op primarily for the benefit of the workers or
as a users' co-op, in which case those people who use it have at least an
equal say with the workers in what goes on. One of the women who
felt like this said:

"Now I think workers' control is fine in a capitalist set up, but when
you're talking about workers' control inside the women's movement,
I don't think you can do that."

Working in a collective, you are much less likely to have unaccept-
able conditions thrust on you than you would in a normal firm because
you still have a say in what goes on.

"I didn't want rules, but a more definite structure, more definitions,
that's something I've learnt, that I wouldn't work in a co-operative
again that didn't have a lot of these things very clearly set out. Not
so that people could be punished for not doing them, but so that
everybody knew what everybody else was supposed to be doing;
because the worst thing about working in a co-op is that nobody
can criticise each other, because you're all meant to be operating on
goodwill, and goodwill doesn't always work at 8 o'clock in the
morning."

WHAT THEY PRINT

As the feminist printers are not just earning their living by providing
their services — though they hope to do this, too — but also see their
work as a political action, they have all thought carefully about what
they will print and how they will charge their customers.

Women in Print prints material not only for the women's movement,
but other stuff that is broadly defined as left, community, alternative.
When we talked to them, they didn't have a totally firm policy, but
tended to discuss issues as they arose:

"When people ring up, it's as important to ask them about the content of their work as it is to find out how long it is. We're trying to
come to some sort of analysis as to whether we should print things
from left groups like the SWP or not, and that involves a lot of
political discussion amongst ourselves to try and get a perspective
on it."

They print some border-line commercial stuff, such as for law centres,
who have a bit of money, to enable them to charge the lowest rates
to women's groups, and so on.

The question of whether to print commercial material is a vexing
one. Apart from the problem that a lot of it is exploitative, racist or
sexist, the feminist printers have to balance feeling that because such

customers can easily get their work printed elsewhere, it shouldn't take up valuable machine time. against sometimes needing that work, either for economic survival or to subsidise their political printing.

Mossside Press have a policy of not doing anything commercial. They also will not print anything that is sexist, racist, or which 'insults the working class':

"We're doing a heck of a lot of women's papers from various parts of the country. That was one of the reasons we started off thinking it would be good to have our own resources. It's taken an awful long time for us to build up that sort of dream come true, having our own machinery and having the power over our own politics.

For the last six months we've been chock-ablock, and a lot of it is women's stuff, which is really nice, because there's no way that was true in the past. I've walked into a left press in the south and they were printing tickets for a police ball. Little things like that gave me a jolt, not just round being a woman, but politically."

Onlywomen differs from the other two in that they are publishers as well as printers, but whilst they are very particular about the material they will publish under their imprint, their printing criteria are less strict:

"We print primarily for women's groups but we would take on other things providing they did not drive us up the wall. There's a distinction between what we print and what we publish. We are prepared to print most things. But most of our printing comes from women's groups and we are happy to get that kind of work. We also do a good deal of commercial printing to make our livings, and we need more. On the publishing side of it, it's quite different — we do have reasons for what we want to publish, we are a radical feminist publishing house."

MONEY MAKES THE PRESS GO ROUND

Like all the alternative enterprises trying to survive in a capitalist society, printers are very conscious of how political decisions are often controlled by financial needs and how their technical operation is similarly constrained.

The hassles Onlywomen encountered from the printers over printing and binding *One Foot on the Mountain* demonstrates the importance of women having control of large machines, as well as ones which can do pamphlets. However, to run such machines requires both skill and money. How do women acquire that skill if they are never allowed access to the machines, and how do they accumulate the money necessary to buy the machines, when at present they scarcely earn enough to pay themselves decent wages? Not everybody feels that *bigger* machines are the solution. *Better* machines would be, but larger ones bring with them a very different kind of job, and dictate different modes of work organisation which people do not necessarily want. This debate will continue in coming years, as typesetting and printing technology become more sophisticated, but also possibly more alienating both for operator and customer. Similarly, another disincentive for buying the large machines is whether they will be given sufficient work to keep such a machine running, because, in order to repay their investment, they need a much higher turnover of suitable work than with the smaller ones. Despite the problems, Mossside now feel economically secure:

"I think we must be one of the cheapest left wing presses in the country, we don't make any profit, but we're not in any debt at the moment. We make enough to pay ourselves a decent wage. It hasn't always been like that, it's been a really hard struggle, there were times when we worked here 24 hours a day and no money at the end of the week, but that's a chance you take. We started off with something like £3,000 debt and none of us had a fucking clue about how to run a business, so we've learnt, it's been a hard struggle."

THE STATE OF THE UNION

There are four shopfloor unions for the print industry — the Society of Graphical and Allied Trades (SOGAT), the Society of Lithographic Artists, Designers, Engravers and Process Workers (SLADE), the National Society of Operative Printers, Graphical and Media Personnel (NATSOPA), and the National Graphical Association (NGA). Everybody we spoke to had only had experience of the NGA, one of those whose roots are as a craft union with long apprenticeships and many of whose members have not adjusted well to the changed conditions in today's industry. The women's presses contain within them everything which the outlook of the NGA has traditionally found most threatening: they are female, part of the network of alternative political presses, and use small offset litho machines which one can learn to run fairly easily.

The NGA has a hard task on to defend the jobs of its existing workers and so it is reasonable for them to insist that all jobs created by government schemes must be paid at the union rate. As Mossside explained, they naturally wouldn't blackleg, undercut or take the bread out of other workers' mouths. But in its turn, the union has trouble understanding that most of the stuff done at alternative presses wouldn't get printed at all if not by them. The union also finds the non-hierarchical collective structure hard to cope with, as it would normally be protecting its workers from their bosses.

Thus, many feminist and alternative presses have found the union largely irrelevant, when it is not being downright sexist and reactionary. Some members talk of not 'diluting the skill', but why should women dilute it more than men? Brenda Philbin, the NGA's sole woman National Officer, said:

"The dilution of skill cannot be denied but can only be attributed to technology and not women. I have heard some male members complain about women's lack of strength rather than skill, in the context of them being prepared to give the same industrial support to.the Association. In fact, it is here that the age-old sexist arguments come into play, e.g. short lengths of service within the Industry and non-attendance at meetings. Of course, the wrong conclusions are often drawn, namely, women not needing to work, not being interested enough to attend and so on. There is no doubt that there is a lot of work to be done within our branches to change some of these myths."

Perhaps what we see here is a discrepancy between official union policy and the behaviour of some branch members. In October 1979, the NGA embarked on a campaign to recruit people employed within the printing industry who were not in membership of any trade union, especially in the white collar area, and they printed a special supplement to their official magazine *Print* about the importance of becoming a broader based organisation. In pursuing this policy, they are currently recruiting more women than men. So, from the viewpoint of its official position, asserting that the NGA is fighting to retain its old craft status is inaccurate. However, the experience of the women we met is a feeling that, at local level, women are most frequently let into the NGA as a last resort — *if* the employer wants to take on a woman compositor and *if* the union can't supply anyone to work the keyboard, *then* they will give her a card, although Brenda maintains that such attitudes are now mainly in the past.

Because the whole print industry is very strongly demarcated, it is very difficult for men as well as women to work their way up through the system. Meanwhile, the majority of women in SOGAT are in Class III (unskilled) where the basic rate is 87 per cent of Class I (skilled and mostly needing apprenticeship). In the NGA, which technically has no classes, there is a small-offset section, where most skilled women members are found, and its basic rate of pay is very roughly equivalent to Class III SOGAT, and is 89 per cent of the full rate for the NGA craft section, where there are few women at present, and hardly any female apprentices. It is impossible to transfer between one part of the industry and another without training or apprenticeship, and whilst this is not the fault of the union, little encouragement or recognition is given to workers who train on the job, which is bound to discriminate against women. Although training and the apprenticeship system are under review, with the existing level of unemployment the major problem for the union now is the lack of job opportunities for everyone.

Nevertheless, things are slowly changing. The NGA how has one national officer who is a woman, although she was transferred over as a result of NGA's amalgamation with NUWDAT, which served the wallpaper industry and had many semi-skilled women and clerical workers among its members. NGA now has 5,000 women members, of whom around 1,700 were previously in NUWDAT, but this development does not directly challenge the NGA's attitude to women as highly skilled craftspeople. However, an NGA delegation attended the TUC women's conference for the first time in 1980 and the national council of the NGA has established a special sub-committee to examine the TUC charter, 'Equality for Women within Trade Unions', and to make recommendations from their findings. A number of these have already been accepted and endorsed by the national council. These are:

1. All branches and officers have been instructed that attempts should be made to negotiate the TUC Model Equal Opportunities Clause into all agreements.

2. The NGA's Education and Training Programme is being modified to give particular emphasis to the problems of women members and the provisions contained within legislation affecting them, e.g. Sex Discrimination Act, Equal Pay Act, Maternity and State Benefits.

3. A request has been issued that branches examine their branch rules to ascertain whether there are restrictions against women members, particularly the 5 year membership qualification for positions on the branch committee or as branch officers.

The national council has also advised branches that there should be positive discrimination in terms of women members to ensure that they are able to play the fullest possible part in the affairs of the NGA. We shall have to wait and see how much these good intentions achieve in practice.

Things also seem to be improving in NATSOPA, whose monthly journal has a women's page, edited by Sue Ledwith. NATSOPA is running a joint creche campaign in the Fleet Street area with the National Union of Journalists, whilst at the magazine company, IPC, it has negotiated a maternity agreement which says that management will not follow any detrimental moves made by the government in any possible future legislation.

For all the reasons we already know, one big problem remains getting women to apply for apprenticeships. The number is increasing — it is now up to 2.2 per cent, which is in line with the numbers in other industries. One other slightly encouraging sign is that the Printing and Publishing Industry Training Board, a body which represents both employers and employees, has commissioned a woman to spend two years researching and reporting on sex discrimination in the industry. Of course, information is not enough, action must follow, but the evidence should provide a lever to help activists campaign for improvements, both in recruitment and training of women.

Because of the importance of getting training and funding for women, Mossside decided to try and get into the union, despite their desire to put their energy into something more constructive:

"The union officials came down, and honestly, it was laughable. The first thing was they wouldn't believe that it was an all-woman set up. There was one bloke who was really against it, but the area officer, he said, I don't think we can refuse, she can obviously print. On machines like the one downstairs they normally wouldn't put a woman down as being a printer, what they'd call her is a 'machine assistant' , and she'd also be given lower rates of pay because of this. When they agreed to me being called a printer, I said: I'd really like this place to become a union shop, and they said, OK."*

This problem of downgrading of women workers is prevalent throughout the printing world, as two of the workers from Mossside discovered when they left there and found jobs in commercial printing. Looking round the industry they realised that there are many women printers

* *The MPG is devoting one of its forthcoming publications to the problems of the print unions, and it will contain a fuller discussion of the interrelated problems of women's position within them.*

who have been doing that job for years, especially in offices. But such a woman won't call herself a printer, her employer won't, and the union definitely won't. One woman got called a Reprographic Technician: "She's a very good printer and prints to a very high standard. She's been printing for many years and is about 50. She runs an offset litho machine and is in charge of the entire print shop. She produces educational magazines, material for teachers and conferences, all stuff written within the organisation. She is paid on some kind of NALGO scale which doesn't bear any relation to NGA wage scales."

Even where women have managed to get into the NGA as printers, generally it is only as small offset operators, and there are very few women in the section covering full craft litho or letterpress machines, and none on those used for printing newspapers. To do that would require retraining in a section of the industry where the prejudices against women are even greater, demarcation even stronger, and the craft tradition even more jealously guarded. It remains to be seen if women will benefit from the technological revolution which is engulfing the print industry, once the excuses of heaviness and night work lose much of their validity.

The NGA claims that it has been trying to unionise offset printshops for several years, but isn't making much progress. This may be because many of the workers see no obvious advantages in joining, while to the union, many of the workers are invisible. They are women and/or they work in some place which, although it has a proper offset machine, has only one or two workers.

In the firm where one of our interviewees works — a non-unionised shop at present, though she's working on it — there are ten employees, of whom only one is a man of 16. Where does this experience lead next? In conflicting directions, it seems:

"The next place I want to work would be in an organised union shop, bigger. I'm really interested in union politics now. And particularly because the NGA is such a shit hole for women. I'm interested in exploring that. I wouldn't say anything as ambitious as doing anything about it — but I might. I've also thought of doing something completely the opposite, like working in a school. Quite a few schools have printing units now, very small and shitty machinery and there wouldn't be much satisfaction or gaining expertise working with them, but I'd be really into having contact with young people, with girls who might never think of working with machinery, but actually might have a lot of interest in technical things."

8
PERIODICALS

The astounding variety of women's liberation activity is perhaps best demonstrated by the range of magazines, newsletters, and journals we have produced, month after month, since the earliest days. New period- icals have been born whilst others have died, but over the last 5 years the number has stayed around 70. Here is recorded the strongest expression of controversy within the WLM and the struggles between it and the rest of the world. Here you will discover the burning issues, the dilemmas and triumphs which keep us all involved. It is a labour of love to transmit the information, the opinions, the message to readerships which vary between 100 and several thousand. With a few exceptions, almost all Women's Liberation publications are produced by the cheapest method — often duplicated — by a collective of unpaid workers, doing it in their spare time. *Spare Rib* is the only magazine which pays its workers, although some organisations, like NAC, pay their workers to put out their newsletter amongst other jobs.. The overwhelming impression is of women producing their magazines because they believe in what they are doing. As somebody from the *Cambridge Women's Liberation Newsletter* put it:

"Why do I do it? I see it in terms of involvement with the Women's Liberation Movement, how involved I want to be. If I come along and find a whole drawer of stuff there, the only thing I want to do is put it in print, so that other women can read it. Especially if I've sieved through it, and there's something really good, I want to get it out to all the other women."

A woman from *m/f*, one of the theoretical journals, explained her enthusiasm in a different way:

"Publishing journals is important because some things will really prove useful and go on, others will work for a period and will be discarded — but as part of something that's ongoing it keeps rolling, and other people are responding and things are happening. I'm not certain that everything we've published is absolutely useful — use- fulness is something that has to exist within a debate."

Different styles, different functions, part of the same broad political movement, and so one must look in several places to experience its rich diversity. Your local newsletter is essential for informing you about feminism locally, there are newsletters which keep you informed about feminism in your job; there are newsletters which provide support and consciousness-raising for some women — black or young or working class or living in the country; and there are newsletters which serve particular campaigns — the National Abortion Campaign, the Women's Aid Federation, Feminists Against Sexual Terrorism. There are magazines and newsletters where specific political tendencies can air their thoughts — the *Revolutionary & Radical Feminist Newsletter*, *Scarlet Woman*, the various women's papers attached to left parties. Other publications try to cross the artificial barriers of a particular political label — *Catcall*, *WIRES* (the national Women's Liberation newsletter). Some are more oriented towards news and information, whilst others concentrate more on analysis — and yet others would argue that you cannot divide the two. There are also several theoretical journals, and *Spare Rib*, our only fairly glossy monthly magazine.

Given the enormous range of periodicals, it is impossible to discuss them all fully in one short chapter, so we interviewed at length women from a small selection of the various types of magazine, and received helpful comments from several others. We chose the *Cambridge Women's Liberation Newsletter* as representative of a small local publication which is duplicated. *m/f* is representative of the theoretical journals which have a book format and are professionally printed, while *Spare Rib* is well-known as a monthly magazine, and makes an interesting comparison with other women's liberation periodicals.

At the end of the chapter there is a list of the feminist periodicals still in existence at the time of writing (February 1981).

LOCAL NEWSLETTERS AND NEWSPAPERS

These are in some ways the most typical women's liberation publications. Though readership is seldom more than a few hundred they are an invaluable channel of debate and information within one area. We interviewed two women from the Cambridge newsletter which, like most of them, is duplicated and produced monthly by a small collective. The only exception to the monthly schedule is the London newsletter which has been appearing miraculously every week almost without a break since 1970. The Cambridge newsletter has also been going since these early days. For a long time it was run by one woman responding to the need for local information with a single duplicated sheet.

The collective of four women who are now running the newsletter has remained stable for a year, but in the past there was a system of rotating responsibility for the newsletter every few months among all the active members of the Cambridge WLM. The collective does little of the writing, and has a policy of no editing or censorship, so their task is to collect everything that women send in for printing, provided it doesn't contravene the seven demands of the women's liberation movement, then to type, duplicate, collate and distribute the newsletter. As well as opinions, reports, poems, musings, it contains certain regular items, such as a calendar, a list of all small group contacts in Cambridge, occasional updating of the telephone tree, the minutes of the last monthly general meeting at the women's centre, progress reports on planning an East Anglia Women's Liberation conference, and the state of negotiations with the council over having to sell the women's centre. Thus, the newsletter in Cambridge is an integral part of the structure of the local WLM. The women who do the newsletter are concerned to make even those women who don't visit the women's centre feel as involved as possible.

Both the women we met are also in the women's centre group. They have been feeling for a while that small groups around Cambridge were becoming more and more diffuse and scattered, and that the women's centre was no longer fulfilling its role as the starting place and meeting ground. Getting small groups to be part of a co-ordinated women's centre is a deliberate policy to pull the WLM in Cambridge together more, and the newsletter has an important part to play in this. When a small group gives a report at a general meeting, it is written up in the newsletter, along with the minutes of the meeting.

However, this is only part of its function, as both women we met felt strongly:

"One of the main purposes of it is that women who felt that they want to write something will be able to do so, and have it published and distributed among feminists, sympathetic women. Like, if you feel particularly mad about something that's happened in the news, or you want to talk about a conference you went to, or you feel very strongly about a particular issue — its a good place to air your feelings. Or if you're doing something in your work which you suddenly find really interesting, you can write about that. For example, Julia wrote about what she was doing at work with microchips and I think a lot of women that had always blocked off about computers and so on found it very informative. Anything you write about will be published."

Because the Cambridge newsletter is the internal organ of the WLM, and is only available on subscription and at the women's centre, not through bookshops, to find out what is going on in women's liberation locally, or even what its ideas are, you must already have had sufficient interest to get yourself to the women's centre, or at least have read about it in *Spare Rib*. In several towns, for instance Birmingham and Manchester, one way out of this dilemma has been to produce two different publications, a women's liberation newsletter as well as a women's paper, the latter being seen as for women who are not necessarily feminists, to provide an alternative to the parodied view of 'women's libbers' so often churned out by the media. The founders of *Manchester Women's Paper* thought they

"would cover many of the topics of interest to women that you might find, for example, in *Women's Own*, but would be looking at them from what we hoped would be a down-to-earth discreetly feminist angle."

Everybody interviewed agreed that there are very different functions to be filled by these two types of paper, and that they are best kept separate, because it would destroy the purpose of the newsletters as they stand to broaden them too much. They would then be serving a completely different function. The woman from *Manchester Women's*

Paper said that its readership

"is more varied than for the *Manchester Women's Liberation Newsletter*, as it should be, and there seems to be quite a loyal readership
who ask when the next issue's due out, but I suspect it still preaches
too much to the converted — 20 per cent of each print-run sells
through Manchester's alternative bookshop alone."

HOW TO START A FEMINIST PERIODICAL

Magazines start in a variety of ways for many different reasons. You
need enough money to print the first issue, reasonable confidence you
can sell how many you print, and the initiative to start. You don't
even need a group to do it, although it certainly helps. Carolyn Brown
explains how she started the (Workers' Education Association) *Women's
Studies Newsletter:*

"I was chosen as a delegate for the 1977 WEA Biennial Conference
and through proposing a resolution on courses for women, tapped
a large well of discontent among women who thought women's
needs weren't sufficiently catered for in our organisation. We held
a breakaway meeting. I took notes and said I'd produce a report.
Someone suggested we have a newsletter to communicate ideas —
I said I'd do it. 'Fools rush in' as they say.

I was high from this conference for about two weeks afterwards
— I'd never experienced anything like it — I'd never been to a conference before in my life. So the first newsletter was produced by me
in a froth of excitement. I eagerly wrote a report of the conference,
collected every other bit of information I could about courses for
women in the WEA and wrote it all out in longhand to be typed and
duplicated at the District office. I called it the *WEA Women's Studies
Newsletter* — not because I knew what womens studies were in those
days! But I thought it sounded descriptive.

I hadn't written anything except the odd letter since I left Art
College in 1968. Talk about rusty! I struggled on a high wave of
enthusiasm. The second issue came out in July 1977, by the third we
had a cover."

Until recently, Carolyn has edited the newsletter more or less single-
handed, which inevitably produced practical strains for her, including
feeling anxious about being seen as individualistic and power-hungry.
As a result of her persistence, national WEA has now taken financial
responsibility for the newsletter, but production is still being sorted
out, so issues no longer appear so regularly.

One way that has been devised to minimise the work and strain of
a publication being produced continuously by one individual or group
is for the production to be rotated amongst the members of its network. This can work quite well when there is a network who keep in
fairly close touch anyway, but such systems have broken down in the
past when commitment has dwindled and nobody else has been willing
to take on production of the next number.

FINDING THE FINANCE

Publications survive on the desire of women to share their preoccupations with others, and the hope that they will respond. One way of measuring the response is whether you can sell enough copies, or preferably subscriptions, to your magazine to recoup your spending. For example, in Cambridge, with a subscription list of about 80, women's subs comfortably pay for all costs of the local newsletter:

"I've just paid a bill for 3 months, for duplicating and paper, which is more or less all its costs, and I think it was £18 for 3 months; that's about average."

But if you want several thousand copies of a printed journal, matters are very different. You need well over £1000 to pay the typesetter and printer for the first issue before you have sold a copy.

m/f tried to get finance from numerous trusts and the EOC. They got absolutely nowhere from all of that, so fell back on raising the money themselves. They each wrote to at least twenty people to ask for initial donations of ten pounds, and raised £500—600 like that and through pre-subscriptions. They put in a certain amount themselves to cover the cost of their first issue. They were fortunate to have well-off sympathisers, and even more fortunate that their typesetters, Red Lion (see Chapter 6) liked the project, so were prepared to do the first three issues at a reduced rate.

All sorts of schemes have been tried to raise money for publications, apart from the obvious donations and jumble sales: *Feminist Review* held a series of lectures at which you paid to hear members of the collective discuss a variety of relevant topics. *Spare Rib* went through a period of having monthly discos — at times mixed, sometimes only women — a source of great debate as well as some money.

We can compare the situation of feminist magazines with that of the commercial glossies, such as *Cosmopolitan*, *Woman's Own* and *Honey*, whose whole rationale is to make profit for their owners. They do this entirely through advertising revenue. This means that circulation figures are paramount, and leads Brian Braithwaite and Joan Barrell, in their book, *The Business of Women's Magazines* to say:

We are not absolutely convinced that very small specialised circulations will ever work in the women's market. Any circulation under 150,000 is not generally viable or particularly attractive as a publishing investment, unless it is in a highly rarified atmosphere as represented by the fashion glossies or something as unique as *The Lady* (p.130).

When the nature of what we are discussing is so different, all we can do is to explain why it is so difficult for feminist publications to reach the vast majority of women, and to feel pleased that we have made as much impact as we have with the minute amounts of money available.

SPARE RIB AND MONEY

Spare Rib was started by seven women who had worked on underground papers such as *Oz* and *Ink*, and wanted 'to put women's liberation on the newsstands'. They set about achieving this with £2,000 (when *Cosmopolitan* was launched in Britain in 1972, the National Magazine Company spent the relatively small sum of £127,000 launching it!) and work roles allocated on a conventional basis — editor, advertising manager, and so on. From an initial sale of 20,000, circulation slumped as low as 5,900 by issue 11, but since then it has grown and developed into the magazine we see today, with a circulation of 25,000 and a collective of 10 full-time and 5 part-time workers.

In the early days *Spare Rib* used to pay contributors, but they had to abandon that as one method of avoiding financial collapse. They would like to go back to paying contributors, but not at the expense of paying the women who work there an adequate wage. The whole question of payment levels produces ambivalent feelings:

"We're torn about paying contributors because a lot of women who say they would like to write for us, but never quite manage it, would then write. But at the same time, I think we all feel we don't want people working at *Spare Rib or* writing for *Spare Rib*, however talented they are, who aren't particularly devoted just because they'd be paid. But at the same time — one woman who was on the collective felt really strongly that as a working-class woman she just couldn't survive on our wages, and unless you had other work, cheap housing, or some kind of subsidy, you couldn't survive at *Spare Rib*.

Another problem is women with children trying to live on a low wage. It does unfortunately restrict the number of mothers who work here."

Spare Rib is also unique among feminist magazines in that it carries paid advertising. It is a necessary but constant source of anguish to find enough advertisers who both think it is worthwhile to advertise in the magazine and will supply suitably non-sexist material. The magazine's latest ploy to raise money is to supply by mail order drying-up cloths, belts, carrier bags, and badges conveying non-sexist messages. At the moment, the magazine seems less likely to collapse financially than ever before. They were even able to weather their last commercial distributor going bust without much panic. In recent times, *Spare Rib* has not needed the large donations of money which had to be put into it several times in the past. This seems to be because the magazine now has a much more solid base in the feminist community:

"I think we stabilised because of the coming together of *Spare Rib* and the Women's Movement in the sense that people who wrote for it became more involved and more people who were previously in the Women's Movement came to see *Spare Rib* as a place where they would write instead of as a kind of liberal cop-out place. Although all that coming together is greatly bewailed by a section of the readership, who seem to think we're miles too man-hating and miles too leftie, miles too radical, I think in fact it gave a really solid base of support for the mag. And as the Movement spread out, we kept growing."

Two factors have helped with this spread. Since PDC started (see Chapter 9), they have handled the radical, alternative and community shops, so that availability in these outlets — sometimes the only outlet in smaller towns — has improved. Also, *Spare Rib* itself makes positive efforts to plug the holes in its distribution by concentrating on a different part of the country about three times a year. They have a regional page where they get women in a particular area to write about what is going on there. This then enables them to do a publicity blitz which combines promoting what women's liberation is doing with increasing demand for *Spare Rib*. They also try to organise a regional readers' meeting to coincide with this. Regional distribution leaves a lot to be desired, so regional pages can hardly fail to make an improvement, although occasionally local feminists have been critical of how *Spare Rib* have covered their area.

FORM AND CONTENT, STYLE AND APPEARANCE

The *Cambridge Women's Liberation Newsletter*, which prints about 100 copies of 10 sides each month clearly requires different production methods from *m/f*, which prints about 2,500 copies of 96 pages twice a year, which is different again from *Spare Rib*, which prints around 25,000 copies of 56 pages monthly. But the question of how a periodical looks, the 'feel' of it, its use of language and graphics, is the result of definite judgements about the image that the periodical wants to convey to its particular readership.

The 'politics of appearance' is something that *Spare Rib* takes very seriously. It has to compete on the newstands every month with the glossy productions of the mainstream women's magazines, yet it wants to be attractive on its own, feminist, terms. In 1977, a group of women who already contributed to the magazine began to meet to discuss the visual content and presentation of *Spare Rib*. The result was the visual issue (no. 72) and an increased commitment to the use of different kinds of images. They want to please readers without trapping themselves with images which either exploit women or give the magazine a knitting-book look. As well as ensuring that feature articles cover a range of subject areas, they also try to avoid repetition of length and appearance. The collective always aims not to have too many words crammed in, but is constantly frustrated by having too much material they can't bear to cut:

"We care a lot about what the mag looks like, although we might not always live up to it. I'm certain that's why we still have photos in by men when we wouldn't have writing in by them. It just seems important to have good lively photos, but there's more women photographers coming along. Nowadays we have more drawings, as our designer is very keen on illustration. I like that — I liked our look before, but it was many more photos than pictures."

Theoretical journals, such as *m/f* and *Feminist Review* have chosen to adopt a fairly conventional format, although *Feminist Review* does make a much greater effort than normal academic journals to include illustrations as an integral part of articles. Both *Spare Rib* and the journals are constrained by economics and practical considerations to use commercial printers. *m/f* explained:

"To do a journal with 2,500-3,000 copies is an enormous job for a small radical printer and many would find it difficult to maintain the quality over a long run like that — that's broadly what I found. So basically, we pushed into the more classic commercial market because there really is a division based on the kind of product you're doing."

At the other end of the technological continuum are the local newsletters:

"Cambridge women's centre doesn't have its own duplicator, but it's not of vital importance because the Bath House (a local community resource centre) only charges us £2 to duplicate per 1,000 sheets. We have to do it ourselves — we type it onto the stencil first, then take it round there and run it off."

How a periodical looks, the printing and the illustrations, is only part of what makes it attractive to a particular readership — what topics are discussed is vitally important, but so is *how* they are discussed. In local newsletters and others which are primarily concerned with relating women's immediate experience, the language is generally direct and personal. Some women use language itself as a consciousness-raising medium — the widely used 'herstory', for example, or trying to exclude any spelling or part of a word which uses 'men', 'man', 'he', 'his', etc. *Spare Rib* uses conventional language, but there are still different writing styles to be considered:

"Everybody has different styles they feel softer or harder on — an article written by an older woman in what someone described as 'Women's Institute' style, I would be quite keen on, because it conveys a different kind of life.

Another woman thinks that *how* things are written is tremendously important and she'd like to experiment more with her own style and she'd like to have more poetic things in the magazine, more daringly written stuff. And maybe also to go out and get more professional writers."

The *m/f* collective is aware that it is widely criticised because its writing is often difficult to understand:

"People demand that one always makes sense, not in theoretical terms, but in common-sense terms, and it seems to me very paradoxical, because of the extent to which feminism talks about the domain of ideology. It seems to me bizarre that anyone should think that language should be so transparent, that clarity at the level of common-sense should be the first demand, because one might stand it on its head and say: that's the first trap, what seems clearest is actually the most problematic, because it's the most internalised.

I think that the demand to write something simply would be relevant if we always knew already what we wanted to say and it was just a question of somehow popularising it or putting it to 'the masses'. We don't see ourselves as doing that, there's no point in saying that we could be sold on the shelves of W.H.Smith, we can't be."

WHO ARE YOU TALKING TO?

m/f doesn't see itself — even potentially — as selling to the mass of women through W.H.Smith, *Spare Rib* does. This is bound to affect their presentation. We have already seen how the *Cambridge Women's Liberation Newsletter* aims to service local feminists and the members of the collective have an extremely clear idea of their readership, even though they don't know everybody personally — a situation that the *Spare Rib* collective must envy at times.

Being Britain's only large circulation feminist magazine, *Spare Rib* is read by a wide variety of women, including some of the 'unconverted'. Its 25,000 monthly sale is small by European standards — for example, in Germany there are two feminist magazines each selling 60,000 — and in comparison to our glossy mass-market women's magazines it is tiny. These are the Jan-June 1980 ABC Total Circulation figures of some comparable titles (rounded to the nearest 1,000):

Women's Weekly	1,649	*Cosmopolitan*	483
Woman's Own	1,608	*Company*	284
Woman	1,512	*Honey*	214
Woman's Realm	765	*19*	184
Woman & Home	706	*Over 21*	126

However, the effect that *Spare Rib* and the whole feminist movement has had on the contents of many of these mainstream magazines gives it an influence far greater than numerical size would suggest.

Spare Rib's aim is to reach all women, but the collective has to assess its present readership, and what they see as the magazine's function. Naturally, in such a large group, opinions vary, though everybody would like to write for the woman who 'isn't a feminist yet' — whoever she may be! The magazine aims to appeal not only to those new to feminism, but also to women who've been involved for a long time, but because of the size of the readership, the collective only have impressionistic ideas of whether they achieve this. There is certainly a whole group of women who read and write for *Spare Rib* very faithfully who are not part of the Women's Movement that is known to the collective — central London or metropolitan — and may not be in any group at all. Reading the letters page, one certainly gets the impression of lots of readers in small towns away from metropolitan areas.

This uncertainty about who reads the magazine and different ideas about its political function and how to fulfil it — a reflection perhaps of similar questions being asked throughout the women's movement at the moment — has led to a lot of self-searching in recent months. The September 1980 issue contained an editorial about their problems with decision-making, which seemed to be about collective working, but were substantially about the magazine's role:

"Should *Spare Rib* get involved in debates internal to the movement — like those raging in local and national newsletters? Or is its function different as a magazine that aims to reach women not yet familiar with feminism? Theoretically most women (at a readers' meeting called to discuss this topic) thought the magazine should open up to controversy. But when concrete examples were mentioned more women expressed the view that *Spare Rib* should enter such debates with caution. Some even thought we should exercise more political control over the letters page."

THE ROLE OF PERIODICALS

When discussing such a wide variety of publications as those which the Women's Movement produces, one cannot generalise about their function, but they all aim towards uniting theory and practice, which is a major aspect of feminist politics. The periodicals we focussed on represent different approaches to this. *m/f*, for example, is specifically designed to develop theory:

"We say *m/f* isn't academic, because while it may be far more difficult and certainly deals with theory, we have a political object which is an attempt to engage in a theorisation of women, the issue of feminism and so on, which is basically about trying to change the position of women which we see as requiring a level of description and conceptual frameworks which are not at the moment available. There's no way in which you can immediately move to another positive position, you've got to destroy what you've been brought up in; if you've been brought up as a psychologist, a sociologist, with an Anglo-Saxon background or whatever, you can't just throw it off, there's work to be done in producing a space in which you can say: This is how I want to look at the question of women. I think *m/f* is really trying to clear that space, and its absurd for people to demand, after three issues, 'Where are the concrete analyses?' I think it's already been pointed out that Rosalind Coward's piece in No. 1 *is* a concrete analysis, as is Elizabeth Cowie's piece on 'Coma' in No. 3."

On the other hand, there are the local and campaign newsletters, who see themselves almost entirely in terms of their usefulness — to report progress, co-ordinate action, announce events, with occasional bouts of reflection on what women are doing. Meanwhile, *Spare Rib*, as suggested above, tries to do a little bit of everything, as it valiantly tries to reflect the divergent politics which make up the WLM. A good example of the sort of debate which continues heatedly within the collective, but which only shows through in the form of finished articles in the magazine, is the question of how racism should be dealt with:

A: "I think I'm in a bit of a minority on the collective but I believe it's important to have critical alliances, if you like, rather than just give women unrestricted access to the magazine to write anything, because I feel that some of the things that black women's groups have written have been quite anti-feminist in the sense of saying: 'Oh, we're not just out for equality under capitalism like all you white women', and I wonder who they have in mind."

B: "I suppose I'm much more on the other side. I feel that I want to recognise what those women have to say, however much I might disagree with some of their politics and their analysis of what goes on in the Women's Movement. Their view may not be correct as I see it, but I'd rather give them the opportunity to say it, because they've organised themselves and attempted to make a statement about racism and their experiences as black women, in the same way, in a way, as we have as white women."

Similar discussions come up all the time in areas such as lesbians and feminism, relating to men, Ireland, economic class, and many more. *Spare Rib* is confronted with the eternal dilemma of being well-known and on open sale in newsagents so that all debates in their pages are very public, and constitute some people's only knowledge of what is going on in the WLM. There are times when we should sort things out among ourselves first, although for *Spare Rib* always to present a unanimous voice with complete answers would also be dishonest.

One attempt to try and solve this problem of having a forum for internal debate, where we could develop theory to guide our practice, and different tendencies could talk to each other, is *Catcall*, an occasional magazine, which is duplicated and has a circulation of about 800. Their collective of three women explained what they are trying to do:

"Our basic aim is to encourage and stimulate the exchange of ideas and the development of theory within the Women's Liberation Movement. We hope that because it is an internal discussion paper rather than outwardly directed propaganda, women will feel free to write down tentative ideas, put forward questions and insights which seem important at a certain time, argue about the role of campaigns and activities.

We do not choose articles according to whether or not we agree with them. This means that we feel it is worthwhile providing a place where women describe their politics and argue with one another, cutting across the lines between the groups talking only to their members or trying to convert everyone else. We would like each issue to contain a range of such articles. . .

We hope that what we print is saying something new, or from a different angle, and that it is written in an understandable way. We don't print personal attacks; articles which are no more than a hackneyed 'party line'; fiction; or reviews (though we would consider these if they were related to a wider analysis)."

THE WRITER/READER

To a feminist publication, the relationship between writers and readers is vital. Because we are all brought up in a society where there is a sharp hierarchy between experts (journalists/theorists) and passive recipients of information, it can take some time to break down these barriers and appreciate that we are all part of the same movement. The producers of most magazines are very keen to get feedback from their readers, so that producing it becomes as much of a participatory act as possible. *Catcall* has been particularly anxious to stimulate this two-way process, but with limited success:

"Our original intention was to hold readers' meetings to discuss particular articles and to get feedback on how the paper was developing. Only one woman came to the first meeting we held, so after that we decided to wait and see if there was any real demand for such meetings. There didn't seem to be. Early in the paper's existence, we called a meeting to discuss writing, and this was quite rewarding.

We do know that different women's groups have discussed several of the articles we have published, and we've had an occasional letter to forward to the writer of an article. But in general we get very little written feedback which indicates how useful or interesting particular articles have been .

Both the *Catcall* collective and individual writers would welcome more response to articles, as well as writing on new topics. It's hard to decide about whether to have a letters page as it can stimulate a response from women who are uneasy with, or don't have the time for a 'proper' article. We didn't have a letter page to start with, but lately we have used extracts from letters where appropriate."

The letters page has always been an important feature of *Spare Rib*, and readers are very voluble about what they think of the magazine and its articles. It is also important as a means of support, as another way of breaking down the notion of simply providing a service. As one of the women from Cambridge explained:

"It is nice to feel appreciated. One woman always tells us what a good job we're doing, everytime she writes in with stuff, which is lovely. It makes you feel good, that you're doing something worthwhile, not just chasing all over Cambridge like a maniac with your stencils."

This is especially important because nobody gets paid for what they do, and often collectives only hear complaints — we are so much better at criticising than congratulating.

WHAT ABOUT MEN?

Feminist periodicals are overwhelmingly written by and for women, but inevitably many are read by some men, and one, *m/f*, allows men to write for them. How do the various approaches fit in with our basic policy that within the WLM we organise separately from men? *WIRES*, and other internal and local newsletters, state that they are for women only, and it is very hurtful to discover occasionally that they have been shown to men, as this shows a fundamental disrespect for our politics.

However, once you extend this principle beyond internal organising newsletters, you are risking that potential readers will not know of your publication because it cannot be obtained in places where men may have access to it. This dilemma is well expressed by *Catcall*:

"We have deliberately aimed to sell the paper within the WLM and for this reason have turned down offers to stock it in 'alternative' bookshops. We hoped that the deliberate limiting of availability would encourage women to express their ideas more freely. On the other hand, it means that in many parts of the country *Catcall* is hard to come by; we need to improve our distribution within the Movement."

We need to know how much what women write (or do not write) is affected by thinking that men might read it, and to distinguish between autonomy as an organising tool and as a way of building our confidence and arguments without men breathing down our necks. We certainly need our internal discussion papers, but we also need more magazines, journals and so on that have the widest possible circulation.

A woman from *Spare Rib* said that they never think of men reading the magazine. However, when describing the relationship of men to the magazine, she said:

"We haven't had an article written by a man for ages, although Andrew Mann of the Children's Book Bulletin has contributed children's book reviews since the early days. The theory is that we would have an occasional one if he had information that no woman did. There were several by men when we started, including George Best. Male readers write quite a lot of letters. I've had some hateful ones from so-called Men against Sexism complaining about how they have been treated. We never print a letter from a man now without bringing it up in a meeting. We get some nice letters from men, saying 'My God, my eyes have been opened'."

There is a shared assumption among all the periodicals we have discussed so far, that politically there is no space in a feminist publication for writing by men, however, the *m/f* collective disagree strongly with this viewpoint:

A: "We've had lots of discussions about how theory 'wasn't male'. One the other hand the question remains of what it means to an author to be male, to be involved in masculinity, and be part of the category of men, the masculine and so on."

B: "It would seem to me to be totally blind to set aside work that is going to be fantastically useful to feminism because of who's done it. There's very little of that work around, which one can really utilise if one wants to re-think the whole notion of men and of women. It seems to me that there isn't much option, if you're faced with something that could be fantastically relevant and useful. For us to say 'no' because it was written by a man would seem to me to be very perverse indeed."

A: "It seems to me fairly clear that editorial control, given any kind of notion of autonomy of feminism, would have to be retained by women. But where the question of men writing comes up, I want to put it in a general background — there are a number of different areas in which feminists as feminists obviously work with men, I see no objection to it, so one can pose this as another area where that question arises. Then I think one would have to say that one's whole notion of what an author is and the relation of an author to a work is such that, as it were, maleness is not going to put its stamp on the text, not in any necessary way. In that sense there are a lot of feminists who write about Lacan, Marx, whoever, and you can be critical of them but they're not out of court because they are men."

There are still very few theoretical journals (three in this country) where women have access for debating issues of importance to Women's Liberation, so it seems unfortunate that *m/f* is prepared to give any of its limited space to men.

WHAT ABOUT THE WORKERS?

A few magazines are run by one woman, for example, the *WEA Women's Studies Newsletter* and *Women Speaking*, our oldest feminist magazine, run since 1960 by Esther Hodge; but most are run by collectives ranging from three at *m/f* and *Catcall* to nearly 20, in the case of *Spare Rib* and the now defunct *Women's Report*. All the periodicals share the work between them as non-hierarchically as possible, and if there is a need for job specialisation, they aim to rotate tasks so that everybody feels involved in it all. Carolyn Brown (of *WSNL*) explained the difficulties of struggling for years without a supportive group:

"Issue after issue, people who offered to do jobs didn't do them properly or took an incredibly long time and had to be reminded constantly. This was all very exhausting and I often ended up spending hours correcting their mistakes or re-doing things.

What could I do? Sit down and explain step by step what had to be done? I felt this would be insulting their intelligence and they would have thought 'She's coming over bossy'. Anyway few of them had the time to stay and talk. I ached for someone to come and talk, read the letters which were pouring in, discuss future articles, exciting possibilities, feminism. But it seemed that though they thought the newsletter was a good thing, it wasn't quite their scene. So I picked up a lot of guilt along the way. Was it my fault we lacked a dedicated group? More and more I ended up doing most things myself. I must point out here that most of the problems occurred on the production side — meanwhile people were really enthusiastic and reliable about writing articles and book reviews — these came from all over the country.

All my problems came to a head when I took a cold hard look at things. Here I was spending 35 hours a week, or more, on a task I didn't get a penny for. This would perhaps have been alright if I'd been a woman whose husband had a 'nice' secure job (and I was content to be supported). But this was far from my reality. My husband's a musician — he might work 4 or 5 times one week, then not at all for the next three. We just about exist on the poverty line through me doing four part-time cleaning jobs.

We had a meeting of people from the WEA branch to discuss forming a collective or approaching our national office for me to be paid. I found this meeting very upsetting and felt that I was under attack. Some people seemed to be suggesting that I'd clutched the newsletter to me — they said they'd had the feeling 'It's your baby'.

At this meeting I kept repeating my dilemma — Yes, ideologically I'd love to form a collective — but who with? Nobody offered. But practically, I need the money, I need to be paid for this, I can't do it part-time and yet do another job.

At the meeting it finally came to a vote and was decided that I should ask the National Office about payment."

The newsletter is now professionally printed, but many of the problems still remain. If there is a group of you sharing the work, some of the problems of lack of money can be alleviated, but to produce a magazine regularly is a time-consuming activity. It often becomes the primary feminist activity for the members of the collective, as most groups meet once a week to sort out what needs doing, offer support to each other and discuss some of the political and personal issues which arise. Then the work of writing, editing, answering letters, admin and production has to be fitted in, too:

"We have an editorial meeting and an admin meeting once a week. All the full-time women do an office day once a fortnight, which means letters, phones, visitors. There is not a clear division of labour but some topics go to a specific person. Some of us are more involved with features, some more with news. Then there are some who do mainly administrative work, although they do some editing too. We certainly don't rotate jobs completely, but there are not many things which none of us could do. Probably only one or two people have ever sold ads or kept accounts. All the women have some administrative task. We don't want only academic-type skills — for some jobs, office experience would be much better.

Then a lot of women are involved in production, i.e. design, pasting up the artwork, proof-reading, co-ordinating with typesetters, bromiders, and printers. Two women are particularly responsible but lots of us help out."

There are five basic elements to the production of any periodical: writing, editing, production, distribution and administration and finance.

Writing is either done by an individual or collaboratively. In some magazines, the collective do little of the writing, for instance the *Cambridge W.L. Newsletter, Spare Rib, Catcall*, whereas *m/f* do a substantial amount of writing. When *Women's Report*, which was a news magazine, existed, all the writing was done within the collective, but this is unusual. Most journals feel they would like to go out and commission work on a topic that is especially important to them, but usually lack the time or money.

Covering news stories in the feminist media forces us to reassess those values that we absorb daily from the rest of the press. How much of what is reported is relevant to women, and if it is, will that fact be obscured by the way it is covered? We cannot change the news slant without us having enough money to employ our own news gatherers — a distant possibility on a big scale, although on a small scale this is already happening, as women send in items to *Spare Rib* about what is going on in their locality.

Editing is often a spill-over from writing, especially when you have a collective like *m/f*, which likes to go through an author's work with them very carefully with discussions and suggestions, as they want to develop a 'distinctive space of argument'. At the other extreme, most local newsletters and *WIRES* publish everything they are sent in, no matter how long or what its style, usually keeping back only something which clearly contravenes one of the seven demands of the WLM or is a personal attack.

If the magazine is written entirely within the collective, then the process of editing clearly begins before decisions are taken about what to write about, but this doesn't necessarily lead to a homogenised approach. In that case, editing is much more of a technical process, to get the number of words to fit into the available space, whereas for most collectives the editorial process is gathering in material from very diverse sources, getting them rewritten over a period, discussing with authors, and *then* trying to fit the words into the space. This inevitably involves political decisions of the sort that have been worrying *Spare Rib* lately — from their September 1980 editorial:

"The other tricky subject — editorial control . . . . Everyone (at the readers' meeting) seemed to agree that *Spare Rib* couldn't just publish whatever comes. The collective have to make choices — more decisions. But fortunately readers seemed to be aware that having that power is exactly what creates the problems. We felt supported in our difficulties, though the problems still hang over us."

Often the dilemmas about editing are as much about what articles you are not publishing as about what changes you make to the ones you do, as on the whole feminists try to be sensitive to the feelings and nuances of an individual woman who has taken the trouble to write something. Most magazines see part of their editorial function as encouraging women who haven't written before, although this can lead to arguments:

"For instance, we sometimes feel women have tried hard, they're expressing a point of view that's important, or they're talking from an experience we haven't dealt with before, and we feel we must print it, even if the article isn't quite what we'd anticipated."

Nearly all of the articles in *Spare Rib* are produced by women just writing in, sometimes with an outline which they are then encouraged to go ahead with. They seldom commission stuff — an important editorial function of most commercial women's magazines — and not more than 25 per cent of any issue is even written by someone from the collective. They get sent about five manuscripts a day, which get passed round among members of the collective for comment. The theory is that articles get chosen by consensus, i.e. everybody has to feel happy about it, but in practice things do get used which members of the collective hate.

All the periodicals which have some selection procedure seem to adopt a fairly similar approach, and have similar difficulties getting the articles they want. *Feminist Review* told us:

"Quite a lot of articles arrive unsolicited, but we spend a lot of time encouraging/soliciting women to write for us. When an article comes in it goes through our procedure. Sometimes we discuss proposals or drafts or outlines with authors before it gets to this stage. On arrival it is given to one person on the collective as its 'article co-ordinator'. She sends it to about five readers, some of whom will be outside the collective and some inside. One person is responsible for 'editorial production' for a whole year, while another is 'editorial continuity co-ordinator' and keeps tabs on what is in and what is expected. In addition to this, each issue has an 'issue co-ordinator' who sort of rounds up the article co-ordinators of all articles selected for that issue. There is also a design team which works with authors on the visual side of their article and liaises with our designer.

The articles are chosen at a collective meeting. The article co-ordinator reports on it, and then we decide by consensus. About twice in our existence we haven't managed to arrive at a consensus view and have taken a vote on it."

Once everything has been edited and/or assembled to the collective's satisfaction the next stage is the *production* process. Again, this is either done within the collective, if it is a question of putting your material on stencils and duplicating and stapling it, or with the help of at least some outside work if it is typeset and printed. Most collectives do at least some of this work themselves, because they need to save money, but also because they want to understand as many parts of the production process as possible. It is this level of participation which is threatened by the rising level of technology being introduced in some parts of the printing industry.

Distribution of the periodical follows printing, and there are various methods of getting it out. In Cambridge, the newsletters are delivered round town by bicycle, in Manchester, the *Women's Paper* is sold in bulk at workplaces by supporters. But the most usual ways to dispose of copies are by subscription through the post and through bookshops, women's centres, bookstalls, conferences, etc. Quite a lot of feminist periodicals do their trade distribution through PDC (See Chapter 9).

The poor woman who deals with subscriptions is a vital part of the *administration* of any periodical. This part of the process is too often neglected in discussing the creative joys of feminist communication, but without people to open the post, answer letters, chase people relentlessly, above all, *make sure the money comes in*, feminist periodicals could not exist.

9
GETTING THE IDEAS OUT: THE PROBLEMS OF DISTRIBUTION

Compared to the effort and energy which has been put into setting up feminist publishers and printers, the efforts to create an independent feminist distribution system in Britain have been relatively limited. This immediately poses the question: do we want or need an independent feminist distribution network? or can we rely on the existing radical network (Publications Distribution Co-op) and established commercial networks? would a feminist distribution network be financially viable? In this context, it is useful to discuss the question of distribution in relation to the distribution of radical material more generally, and to compare the situation in Britain with that of other countries. (Two of MPG's earlier publications, *Where Is the Other News?* and *The Other Secret Service*, deal specifically with the forces which operate to keep all alternative magazines off the newstands, and what the French government has done to rectify a similar situation there.)

There are two main related aspects of distribution. Firstly, that of the network itself: how do feminists get their work distributed? and secondly, outlets: to where does feminist literature get distributed?

SPREADING IDEAS: IS IT ONLY SUPPORT WORK?

Without an effective and efficient distribution system, which ensures the work women produce will reach its audience, all the sweat and labour that goes into producing books, pamphlets, magazines and so on, will be fruitless. Unfortunately, the question of distribution, and availability more generally, is frequently ignored or regarded as a secondary issue. Perhaps it is because distribution is seen as the less 'glamorous' side of publication. Perhaps also it has something to do with the fact that distribution in our society means, is identical with, *selling*. There is a certain distaste on the part of the radicals in Britain to indulge in this form of activity. There are two factors that contribute to this reluctance. One is the moral ambivalence towards and theoretical confusion about the role of money — should socialists or feminists sully their fingers with this most capitalist and patriarchal of objects? Secondly, there's a certain middle-class snobbery towards commerce of any sort. It's better to be a (high-status) producer of ideas than a (low-status) purveyor of someone else's.

Further evidence of this reluctance is seen in the fact that until very recently, feminists did not have their own independent publicity agency, to bring their publications to public attention. This has now been rectified by the setting up of a one-woman publicity business, Ultra Violet Enterprises.

Distribution, in relation to the actual production of literature, is largely seen as support work, necessary, but not the most vital or important of tasks. The fact that on the left generally distribution is seen as of secondary importance to production is reflected in the fact that it is only in the last ten years that there have been independent radical bookshops, and a distribution network for only four years.

As far as feminists have been concerned the question has been a peripheral one. The one attempt to provide a solely feminist distribution network was combined with a feminist publishing enterprise (Feminist Books), and when the publishing side stopped for lack of capital, the distribution function also ceased. This is not a criticism of Feminist Books but an illustration of the general lack of enthusiasm for such a project.

The one other attempt made more recently to have women's material distributed by women has been the Women's Liberation Bookbus. This began in 1977 and is run by a small group of feminists who try to make feminist literature available in small towns and villages where there is no bookshop or other means of access. In their pamphlet describing their work, they express the hope that what they do will encourage other women to set up similar ventures in other regions. As far as we know, this has not happened.

In the bookshop arena too, there are relatively few independent outlets, in the whole of Britain there is only one bookshop which specialises in women and that is Sisterwrite in London; this compares with between 20-30 women's bookshops in West Germany and twelve in France. West Germany has its own independent feminist distribution network — Frauenbuchvertrieb — which has been in operation for five years, distributing books, pamphlets and magazines with a distribution list of about 100 titles.

Until recently there was an independent feminist network in the USA — Women in Distribution (WIND), which handled 400 books, records and graphic items but this has now folded up.

In Britain, therefore, the means of distribution and numbers of outlets for women's literature remains largely confined to the one major radical distribution network, PDC, and to alternative bookshops. Other outlets of significance are women's centres and bookstalls at meetings and conferences. All these cater largely to an audience which is already aware of the existence of feminist and other alternative ideas.

The other means of getting the material out is through commercial distribution networks, but these normally cater for publishers with a comparatively large turnover and not for smaller fry. Hence the Women's Press are distributed by Macdonald & Evans, while Virago uses Routledge & Kegan Paul. Sheba Press and Onlywomen both use PDC. *Spare Rib* uses PDC for radical bookshops, but its newsagent distribution is handled by Comag, a national commercial magazine distributor. Some feminists may be sceptical or suspicious of using commercial networks but the fact is that it can make a huge difference. For example, the sales of *Camerawork*, a radical photography journal, rocketed during the short time it was taken on by W.H.Smith, and fell sharply again when Smith's refused to take it any longer.

PDC

The question of whether to use existing commercial facilities or to set up independent systems of its own is a general and fundamental political question for radicals. The Publications Distribution Co-operative is the major radical alternative distribution network in Britain, handling about 90 periodicals and 33 journals over the whole range of feminist, socialist, radical and alternative movements. Several feminists became involved with PDC at its beginning, and pushed for the importance of feminist literature, and from the outset it has sold very well. Feminist literature is now much more widely available because of PDC, and its very existence has encouraged other developments such as new bookshops and more self-published books. Bookshops know that they can get a wide selection of alternative material on a regular basis, and writers know that their material will be distributed.

PDC has survived as a political venture because it has been able to subsidise cheaper publications and those with low volume sales with higher priced and comparatively popular books and periodicals. Using PDC is a fine balance of political and financial considerations which, given the precarious nature of institutions sympathetic to feminism, should not be taken lightly. Many women were dismayed when *Feminist Review* left PDC after four issues to be distributed by Pluto Press, a socialist publishing house which has begun to publish some feminist books. Pluto was possibly encouraged by the evidence of increased sales of feminist material which was stimulated at least partly by the existence of PDC in the first place.

PDC is not of course an all-woman enterprise, and it is a matter for political debate among feminists as to whether this matters, and if it does, to what extent?

SISTERWRITE BOOKSHOP

Sisterwrite is the only bookshop in Britain which specialises in women's books. They have now produced their own mail-order catalogue to widen their market beyond North London, and approximately 2,000 copies of it have been sold.

The bookshop opened in November 1978. Two of the three members of the collective had had some previous experience in the book trade. As one of them said: 'It just came at that point as the inevitable next step.' They had surprisingly little trouble in setting up the shop. A number of women provided interest-free loans and they found someone who could afford to buy the premises; he is now their landlord, but they have the option to buy the place, which they are currently pursuing.

Of the books they stock, nearly all are written by women, although they will stock books by men on subjects about which very little has been written, or books which are reference or historical material. The wide range of stock means that while virtually everything is by or about women, it's not all feminist; but they will usually only stop taking a book if they get feedback from women that the book is offensive or in some way denigrates women. They will order any book that a woman requests without exception, however. Their stocking policy is consciously and deliberately a liberal one, they stock material which is not just politically 'feminist', but also material from many different kinds of female experience.

The commitment of the collective to the shop extends beyond just running it on a commercial basis, and they see it as a wider resource centre for the community. The Women's Research and Resources Centre occupies the upper floor of the building, and there is now a reading room. They want to develop a foreign language section, and they want to reprint articles and pamphlets which they feel are important. They would also like to encourage meetings and poetry readings in the evenings, and they intend to start making visits to schools in order to publicise their stock to teachers and younger women.

The collective were insistent that the bookshop would not exist without the existence and support of the WLM:

"The thing we've always implied and which never comes out in what's been written about us is that it exists *because* of the Women's Movement, it doesn't exist in a vacuum."

OTHER WAYS OF SELLING: MAIL-ORDER AND BOOKCLUBS

There are two main reasons why publishers set up bookclubs or operate a mail-order system. Firstly, they are able to offer their books to customers at a reduced rate, since the books are sold direct and not through an intermediary; secondly, they are able to reach a wider audience, some of whom may not have access to a bookshop or decent library.

The first feminist bookclub was set up by The Women's Press in September 1980 and already has almost 1,000 members. It hopes to put an annual selection of 50 books within the reach of women who wouldn't normally go into a radical bookshop, and recent titles have ranged from a novel by Collette to short stories by Doris Lessing to The Women's Press' own *Why Children?* Membership costs £5 a year. The club's aims are to make money for the Press' own publishing programme, to increase sales of books they think are important and to encourage more people to buy books (both from the Press and other publishers) by offering discounts of between 25-50 per cent.

Some people argue that bookclubs take away trade from both bookshops and distributors such as PDC, as both are by-passed when books go direct from the publisher to the reader, at a much reduced price. One of the Sheba Press collective expressed this view:

"A bookclub involves selling other people's books as well as your own, which is a great disadvantage to women's bookshops, and to the distributors for that matter. . . . I personally think that it's important to support the whole idea of alternative distribution like PDC, which would be cut out."

When Sheba Press started up, they began operating a mail-order system, by which people could buy their books from them direct, although they do not sell other publishers' — this being the difference between mail-order and bookclub. Sheba did this to raise capital to get started; people would pay a certain amount of money beforehand to get the books at a reduced rate when they were published. When they proposed this scheme, Sheba approached Sisterwrite bookshop to discuss whether this would be competing for trade, and they agreed that it would not.

But is it the case that direct selling by publishers works against other forms of selling? Bookshops, for instance, like libraries, are used by a fairly well-educated minority; it could be argued that bookclubs reach people who otherwise would not use either libraries or bookshops. They are certainly useful to women in areas where there are few bookshops or with limited library facilities. A *Bookseller* article quoted the director of a publishing company which operates a bookclub as saying:

"In no way is the market for books diminished by clubs. Consumption is extended. People choosing to buy in this way are probably not habitual bookshop customers. As bookclubs flourish, so do bookshops. (*Bookseller*, 26.7.80)

If feminists and socialists want to work in a complementary way with each other, and not end up competing — or at least thinking they are — we should be much more knowledgeable about who uses what types of outlets, and also why those who *don't* use them, don't. The arguments we have met over outlets and their users have been largely based on assertion. In our researches into library use, for instance, it became clear that there was no information which could allow us to make any generalisations about who used or didn't use libraries. We know of no large-scale studies on this, and the smaller ones are too geographically specific to be generalisable. It would be useful to have a few more facts, such as the ratio of women to men users — nowhere has the evidence been more contradictory.

PUBLIC LIBRARIES

There are 15,000 branch libraries in Britain, divided up into 140 library authorities. Traditionally they have been very insular, assuming that they have a service to provide for the people who come to use them, and that these will always be a minority of the population — as indeed they have been. Until recently, libraries did not put themselves out to attract a larger public, their range of services was fairly narrowly defined and their attitude more than a little elitist. It was noted however by Ward (1977):

. . . while books and libraries are physically available to all, they are mentally inaccessible to many, as equality of opportunity is not matched by equality of expectations. (p. 87)

Librarians as a profession have been notoriously uninterested in finding out why people *don't* use libraries and finding ways to attract more people to use the facilities provided.

In the last few years, some libraries have made efforts to break down the barrier between themselves and a wider public. Not only have many of them promoted links between themselves and adult education — by providing film-shows, poetry readings and exhibitions on their premises — but a few have also instituted an 'outreach' policy, where library materials are taken out into the community rather than waiting for the public to come to them.

In the London Borough of Lambeth for instance, they take materials to playgroups, day nurseries, women's groups, prison aftercare and local evening classes; and in 1974 they organised a special exhibition of feminist books with its own catalogue which toured the borough.

The question of what to stock can be a vexed one. In Lambeth, unlike many library authorities, they do have a criterion for selecting materials. This involves recognising material which contains harmful stereotypes (particularly race and sex stereotypes), and weeding out those whose attitudes are offensive and actively seeking materials which combat these stereotypes:

"Naturally, our stock does not consist entirely of non-sexist and non-racist material, but we are trying to eliminate the most blatant examples of racism and sexism."

The librarian we spoke to was asked what range of material she would like to see aimed at women, since she felt that much of the feminist material available at present was too difficult for many women to tackle, because it makes a lot of assumptions and presumes knowledge that most women don't possess:

"I'd like to see more feminist material aimed at young women in their teens. There are many feminist youth workers now who could use such material. There is a particular need for suitable material on women's health, the body and sex. By developing pride and confidence in young women themselves, youth workers can then develop the theme into talking about sex roles."

Lambeth libraries are now liasing with the Lambeth Girls Project, a scheme set up by feminist youth workers to develop the separate identity of young women in youth clubs which are often dominated by young men and male youth workers. The library authority has been able to make a positive contribution to this group, being represented on the management committee and supplying the youth workers with suitable materials and information.

OTHER LIBRARY AND INFORMATION SERVICES FOR WOMEN

Much work remains to be done in the public library service, which must be struggled for despite public expenditure cuts. Pressure can be applied both by feminist library workers and women who use the services. But sometimes, the most effective way of achieving what you want, particularly if it is a highly specialised service, is to set up your own organisation. We are including brief reports on the library work of the WRRC, the Feminist Archive, and the Fawcett Library, as well as the Equal Opportunities Commission which, being a government-sponsored body, is an important source of information about women. Unfortunately we were not able to interview them.

THE WOMEN'S RESEARCH AND RESOURCES CENTRE

From small beginnings in a damp basement in Gower Street, London, the WRRC has grown, and its activities now cover a Research Index on over 500 research projects, a bi-monthly newsletter for its members, and it acts as a meeting place for feminist academics. It has organised a feminist summer school and is planning another; it also publishes pamphlets (see Chapter 4). The library holds well over 1,000 books, 500 pamphlets, 500 partial and complete sets of periodicals and 100 unpublished research papers.

The Centre now has charitable status. It is run by a collective which has overall responsibility for policy, but it is staffed by three part-time paid workers who are responsible for the day-to-day running of the Centre and the library. Originally they had a librarian who was sponsored for a year by the EOC.

A large part of the Centre's work is concerned with answering queries; they receive over 100 every week, ranging from school students doing projects to doctoral students. They also get queries from people outside academia who want information on a vast range of subjects relating to women. An innovative part of the WRRC's work has been the devising of a feminist classification system for its collection.

The new classification system has to take two contrary factors into account. Because the Centre cannot rely on the expertise of the librarian all the time, the system has to be simple enough to grasp it easily. But it also has to be sufficiently flexible (i.e. complex) to deal with the different subjects under which the material is classified. There are similar schemes in operation in America and Sweden, but so far the idea is not widely accepted in this country. But for an attempt at combatting sexist indexing and cataloguing see Joan Marshall's book *On Equal Terms.*

THE FEMINIST ARCHIVE

The Feminist Archive is a newly-established collection of women's work based in Shepton Mallet in Somerset. It hopes to be the prototype for a regional network of centres

"devoted to documenting the living herstory of the Women's Movement and maintaining national and international contacts for exchange of material and information."

The Archive is now looking for new premises and a group of women in the provinces to take over running it.

The materials it deals with are wide ranging, and include unpublished research, and ephemera such as badges, posters, calendars, song sheets and conference papers; there are also books and periodicals. The Archive intends to place particular emphasis on regional material. Future plans include collection of phonograph records, audio and visual tapes, cine and micro film and a costume gallery. It is also hoped to build a collection of personal papers and original manuscripts of writers, artists and politicians.

There is at present no money for acquisitions, so the Archive is dependent upon donations, and women are asked to send stuff that they think might be appropriate. They will place restrictions on the

CITY OF LONDON POLYTECHNIC

BIBLIOFEM

The Joint Library Catalogues of the
Fawcett Library
Equal Opportunities Commission
together with a Continuing Bibliography
on Equal Opportunity and Women

availability of material if donors wish it to be seen by women only, since men will be allowed to use the facilities.

THE FAWCETT LIBRARY AND BIBLIOFEM

"The Fawcett Library is the largest and most comprehensive source of information on women in the United Kingdom, if not the world." This is the claim of the staff of the Fawcett Library now housed at the City of London Polytechnic.

The library was built up as a collection of books and information for the members of the London and National Society for Women's Service — now the Fawcett Society — and was formally inaugurated as a library in 1926. Its contents reflect the wide scope of the interests of its members, many of whom were prominent in British social and political life, thus the collection includes material which has no direct reference to women. While most of the collection relates to British affairs, there are holdings of European, Arabic and Japanese materials. It's roots being in the Suffrage Movement, the library has much material on this issue, as well as books on prostitution, women's employment and education. Other fields covered are unionisation, sexology, marriage, the family, law on women, arts, religion and fashion. It also contains several specialised collections, personal papers, photographs, press cuttings and periodicals.

This wide range of material obviously has to be meticulously classified and catalogued, and a computer-based cataloguing system — BiblioFem — has been developed. BiblioFem is a joint catalogue of the Fawcett Library and the Equal Opportunities Commission in Manchester. The Fawcett Library provides the historical material while the EOC's holdings are largely current information. The inclusion of both into a joint catalogue is a valuable and vital resource for anyone concerned with women's issues.

THE EQUAL OPPORTUNITIES COMMISSION INFORMATION CENTRE

The EOC was set up in 1975 after the Sex Discrimination Act was passed, to promote the equality of opportunity between men and women and to work towards the elimination of sex discrimination. The main office is in Manchester, with offices in Cardiff, Glasgow and London. It was decided to set up an information centre, as opposed to simply a library, which would contain not just books but also a range of other materials including government reports, statistics, *Hansard*, press cuttings, slides, sound and visual recordings, posters, badges, cards, and so on.

The Centre, which opened in 1977, offers other services apart from the catalogue (see above). It has a specialised enquiry service to deal with specific aspects of legislation such as employment or education, and a register of research to record the network of people known to be interested in the field. This will enable people to contact others who are working on related interests to their own. The service is public, and is thus open to both men and women.

Future possibilities include a loan service to teachers of material to

BOOKSELLER AND PUBLISHER

any women only start looking for a position when necessity forces them to.

This is to be regretted, as there is very little choice in positions and moreover, most are humbly paid due to the lack of preparation.

Bookselling especially requires a training of many years' standing.

There is no inherent objection to this profession for women, it is very suitable for them. Her commonly greater proficiency in language than men, and her greater precision, can be a great asset.

As the largest part of the reading public consists of women, it is very much to be regretted that only men are in a position to judge the worth of a book written by a woman's hand. It is common knowledge that those books which have been widely acclaimed and which were written by women, passed from one publishers' to another without these male arbitrators realising their worth.

A woman-author would have immediately foreseen the success the book would have and a woman-publisher with literary taste and knowledge as well.

From: Professions for women,
by Johanna van Woude, Amsterdam 1899

Feministische Uitgeverij Sara
Plantage Muidergracht 149
1018 TT Amsterdam
Telephone 020-243156

help classroom discussion about equal opportunities; there will also be increased emphasis on development of non-sexist children's books and teaching materials.

10
SEXISM IN
THE RADICAL
BOOK TRADE

So far we've concentrated on women's struggle for survival, either in the financially starved but politically vibrant autonomous feminist groups or in the blatantly commercial world of capitalist book production. However, significant numbers of women are also trying to survive in an important area which lies between these two — working with men committed to radical politics and radical books. A number of the women we interviewed work with men for whom fighting sexism is part of their stated political practice, yet all the women expressed some level of hostility at the way they had been treated.* The problems are the same as those encountered in other parts of the industry — women denied access to skills, to the decision-making processes, and to financial responsibility, feminism denied or diminished as a political force, books from the Women's Movement used cynically to make money. What makes it harder to bear here is that our expectations are higher, because everybody involved maintains they are doing it out of political commitment, and we are more disappointed than usual when practice fails to live up to theory:

"What infuriated me most was the hypocrisy, they said one thing, whilst doing all the things that any straight publishers would do; they were exactly the same and yet they hid behind a facade of being an alternative, socialist press. They treated the women in the press no differently. But the thing that was so upsetting was, having gone into a situation where I felt that people were going to accept and understand things, where I would be encouraged, I discovered that, in fact, they were as narrow and naive and chauvinistic and patronising as in any other straight organisation."

AFTER THE REVOLUTION AFTER ALL?

For feminists who go to work in radical organisations, the dilemma is not entirely one of entrenched sexist behaviour, it is also connected with the larger political question of the relationship between socialism and feminism.

"The compromises that exist when you go to work in a socialist publishing house as a committed feminist are that Crimson is organised on very conventional male-left lines and I am totally antagonistic to male-left ways of organising, which doesn't mean I'm not a socialist, but it does mean that I cannot cope with the contradictions which continually arise between what I want to see happening as a feminist and what Crimson wants to see happening as a socialist publishing house."

Although such contradictions may be theoretically based, for example, over the differences between how the men and the women would analyse the class position of women, and this then being reflected in the contents of books, in our experience, because feminists believe theory and practice are inseparable, most of the problems of working in mixed radical groups are practically expressed. The women in one bookshop collective decided they couldn't sell women-only publications because some of the men they worked with wouldn't respect women's privacy. They also couldn't get the men involved in the campaign to put stickers on sexist and racist book covers, nor to challenge publishers about their sexism, because the men did not want to antagonise the publishers.

Being in the WLM provides us with a political framework for understanding people's behaviour in terms of power relationships, and when we look at the radical book trade, the same patterns emerge as elsewhere in society — no radical publisher in Britain except the feminist presses has a full-time woman commissioning editor, women in bookshops are rarely involved in negotiating the lease or being responsible for maintaining the premises, female authors are often restricted to 'women's issues'. Part of a feminist analysis is to believe that making people aware of such problems is a step towards changing them, and that changes in our practice now are essential for long-term improvement. When confronted with men who do not accept that there is anything wrong with current practice, it is easy to see how conflict can arise, particularly as loss of power is usually involved.

"I don't think you can say you *are* a radical press if you do not actually work in a way which is radical . . . The ultimate contradiction is that they publish feminist books which spread feminist ideas, but when those ideas come filtering through their front door they don't like it. They found it so threatening at Radical Press that they made life very difficult for the two women, so that both of us have left."

DEMOCRACY AT WORK

Of course, it's not only women who have no control over their work. It's that being a feminist makes you more aware of it, you notice that the men are most often in the position of control, and your political practice makes you conscious of work being structured in a more male-defined way:

A: "The final decision about which books to order always lay somewhere else, basically with the man who was the manager, which was very frustrating when you'd built up a lot of research and you did have very definite ideas about what to sell. I think what really frustrated me was that the economic decisions were taken somewhere else again, in other words, someone else decided that we shouldn't have as much stock at a particular time, and you didn't have access to everything that went to make up that decision. At Sisterwrite we follow the whole process all the way through, we do the accounts and we know what happens to the invoices, whereas there you'd unpack the books, take out the invoices and they'd go somewhere else, and you didn't know the whole process."

B: "I can remember times when stock would have to be run down because of supposed overstocking and you weren't allowed to buy books. But when you disagreed and the shelves were empty and you couldn't re-order any more books, that was frustrating because it almost made your role of providing that service redundant. But there is no way that could happen here (at Sisterwrite) because we have control over our own priorities."

Significantly, more of the radical typesetters, printers, and book-shops aim to work collectively and non-hierarchically than the publishers, and we wondered why hierarchical organisation among the publishers seems to be so prevalent. Those who control them might point to the greater range of skills required or the higher initial financial investment needed to start them (though when you think of the cost of modern printing and typesetting machines, this argument seems less valid), but might it also be related to the fact that in terms of prestige, publishing is further up the hierarchy than the other forms of employment?

"The owner of my firm does have the controlling say, but from what I can gather from other radical publishing, it's less hierarchical in some ways than other places. There are a lot of meetings to discuss what goes on. I only participated in those meetings for a short time, but often I wondered why I was bothering. I felt it was the acceptable face of radical publishing, that the real decisions were not being made there and that it was a window-dressing to keep the natives quiet. Towards the end I started not going because I didn't want to have to sit there and listen to my boss pontificating, or to collaborate in the use of those meetings to pretend that there was no hierarchy. It was so obvious that there *was* a hierarchy — and who was at the bottom of the shit heap? Me. Basically editorial control is the key. If you're not prepared to let anyone else edit your books — or decide at the end of the day what books you publish — that *is* a hierarchy and they could never understand that. On another level he also used to say: 'Well, I bear the financial burden, therefore at the end of the day, *because* I have to bear the responsibility, I have to make the decisions.' So the two levels would go on simultaneously and depending on which hat you caught him with, that was the answer you got. The fact was that the men were at the top of the hierarchy and the women were at the bottom of it. Who was it who had a strong feminist consciousness at that time? The women office workers."

This experience was very similar to that of another woman:

"The owner generally has the last word, in that he has the power of veto; because it's *his* money that started Radical Press. In fact, when it comes down to it there's no say but his. What I'd been led to believe was that Radical was a co-operative or collective situation. In fact, what happened was that it was made blatantly clear — he actually said this — that only the two senior men talked because they were the only people who had anything to say. So we kept our mouths shut because we were generally made to feel pretty stupid. Sue kept her mouth shut out of choice because she felt so frustrated that she was in this situation. She's a very strong feminist in a situation where she was doing a female role in publishing, but also trying to push the feminist books, and where she was told by the men that feminism wasn't very important. Then right at the bottom of the scale came Mary and I. I could type, which was disastrous, as I simply got a typewriter stuck in front of me, and then I got landed with cleaning the office because no-one else bothered to do it — and it was made obvious, even by Sue, that I was in the lowest position so I should be the one to clean up."

PUTTING US IN OUR PLACE

In a hierarchical and competitive atmosphere, solidarity among women can easily be undermined in the individual struggle to retain one's self-esteem. In the firm where these women worked, their contributions were persistently underrated, and the workers were given no proper job definitions, so that whatever they did could be criticised:

"I started doing cash flows, to be told that if I added one and one it wouldn't make two; which was absolute rubbish because I'd been doing the cash flows beautifully for three months and I made one mistake and he used it as a way of keeping me off-balance. On another occasion, Sue spent five days doing a poster, but because the owner had told her wrongly how the printers set out the plate, she did about £400 worth of work for nothing. So she was totally exploited and at the same time made to feel like a silly hysterical woman when she'd told him beforehand it was wrong."

A frequent complaint was the lack of training and guidance given to women when they start, a tactic frequently used in the commercial business world. It reinforces the initial lack of confidence many women feel, and is then used as the means of exploiting us, having demonstrated our supposed inferiority. Two women in different firms were told they were bad editors on the basis of having copy-edited one book, which they undertook without anyone giving them any guidance beforehand about what was required.

"This feeling of being underestimated was one of the things that frustrated me right at the beginning — if someone really does think you are stupid, after a while, you're going to *behave* a bit stupidly in their presence, unless you're very strong and self-possessed. After being there for six months I felt I had to leave because I felt my whole self-esteem was being chiselled away. From going into it feeling: 'Well, my mind's working, I'm fairly intellectual, I know where I'm at, I'm beginning to learn about the things that are important to me, for instance, feminism', I got to feeling so stultified and in a straight-jacket. All my creativity had gone out of the window, I was vegetating."

It surely cannot be a productive work situation when people's talent and initiative are allowed to atrophy in this way, or when they are driven into outbursts of impotent rage, yet these are tested patriarchal methods of retaining control:

"My reaction to my boss's behaviour was to wait until I was so angry that I'd turn round and very coldly say something. He would brush me aside, as if I were a silly little girl who didn't know much better. The other woman would get so angry she'd get hysterical and start crying, she couldn't hold it in, she'd be so angry with him. I felt it was exactly what he wanted because he then had us in a totally controlling situation. . . . I don't understand how he could reconcile that with being a socialist."

SEXUAL HARASSMENT

Another traditional way of oppressing women at work is by sexual harassment, and it is sad to report that even so-called socialists are not immune from this despicable practice:

"Two weeks after I arrived, I began to be aware of the fact that he was being very smarmy to me, he would come up and put his arm around me — it was incredibly uncomfortable, he was making very obvious sexual advances towards me. He offered me a lift once or twice and, on one occasion, I accepted and he made very obvious advances. I said, 'Stop the car,' and I got out and from that moment on, I was no longer OK. He'd make continual sexual points; if a woman walked into the room he'd say: 'She's got nice legs' or 'She's sexy' or 'She's horrible' or something. The women in the office were continually being provoked into a reaction."

Fortunately, sexual denigration by so-called radicals is rarely so overt, though some women might wonder why we are at all surprised by it. It is distressing that whilst behaving like this, men can continue to make money and a reputation by publishing books by feminists, some of which are very important. All the authors who want to write about what's happening in this area have to go to such publishers, because commercial publishers are often unwilling to publish their work. What is so frustrating is that they're good feminist titles, yet some of the radical publishers have no conception of what feminism is. They have no intention of changing the way they oppress women, either, while continuing to benefit greatly from the intellectual and financial blindness of the rest of the publishing industry.

Up to now, such cases have not been made public, as feminists are as worried as other women by what will happen if we do: we doubt whether we will be taken seriously, perhaps people will think we are exaggerating; maybe other men will say we brought it on ourselves by acting provocatively, and maybe — most upsetting thought of all — our male comrades will tell us that even if it is true, it does not affect the fact that good work is being done, that it is not a significant factor in anyone's right to be thought of as a radical publisher, so please will we keep quiet about it, and stop making a fuss.

SUPPORTING OURSELVES

In many radical firms, as well as in trade unions and more conventional workplaces, women are finding that forming a women's caucus helps to break down the isolation. These function in a variety of ways. In one bookshop the meetings are sporadic, but important:

"We are all feminists, and our meetings have enabled us to get to know each other better; to co-ordinate our work in the bookshop with our involvement in the women's movement locally and nation-ally; to let off steam about our work; to feed into the collective positive suggestions for improving the way we work together; and, far too often, we spend time telling one or other of us that she does make a valuable contribution to the shop, that it is possible for her to cope and that she should stick with us and help us change our way of working to suit our needs."

There are also a variety of women's support networks which meet spasmodically to provide energy between women from different work-places, e.g. feminist librarians, women printers (see Appendix).

SO WHY WORK WITH MEN?

In deciding to work with men, feminists are clearly making a political choice at that point in their lives not to put all their energy into women-only enterprises. The reasons are usually a combination of pragmatic and political. For example, in most towns in Britain the community can hardly support one radical printer or bookshop, let alone have separate feminist ones and there are no women locally with the necessary skills. As men have most of the financial resources in this society, our best chance of diverting some of it for our purposes is to be in there, fighting for it.

However, our reasons for choosing to work as feminists in mixed organisations can sometimes be stated more positively. One woman felt strongly that we should try and educate half the population. She did not feel she could turn her back on men, because we have to carry on working with them. She left her job in a radical press because of the impossibility of making an impact. Yet:

"It's only since I've left that I've thought that as women in publish-ing, we've got to change things. . . . I don't know how we can, because I couldn't do it when I was there."

Another woman said:

"I don't think I could ever be a separatist, but my highest priority is changing women's attitudes, not men's, and an awful lot of women work with men and a lot of women can only be reached through the means men have to offer. I'm very much in favour of using the feminist presses as much as possible, but they haven't got endless money or resources. I think that men will change, but they won't change because we plead with them, they'll change because they have to, because we turn our back on them and show we can do it without them. This attitude has got me into a lot of trouble at times when I've been seen as vey uncompromising — my attitude to men is very ambivalent."

WHERE ARE THE WOMEN EDITORS?

So long as feminists carry on working with men, we cannot entirely avoid the task of trying to change their consciousness, for even though we may feel it is not our job — and a thankless task it is anyway — at the same time there are principles to be established and our own life to be made more bearable. Having been slower than some commercial publishers to start publishing feminist books, the socialist houses are now starting to do so, partly because of pressure from their own women workers and the belated realisation that the Women's Liberation Movement is not a diversion from *real* politics. A more cynical view is that they suddenly noticed a corner of the market which sells well:

"They won't publish a really radical feminist book that slags off men because it would be too threatening to them, but they will publish socialist feminist books which more or less fit into their accepted view. The exception to that would be if they found a book they thought was so good they could make a lot of money out of it."

Such feelings arise partly because of the absence of any feminist editors at decision-making level, which causes frustration and political misunderstanding:

"My firm have finally got themselves sussed enough to work out that there are actually one or two topics in the universe where you can't have a man's name on the book cover. They realised that sexual harassment, for example, might be one of them; so then the discussion moved on to who would edit it. And I said that I didn't think that any woman whose politics I trusted to write this kind of book would allow herself to be edited by a man. But nobody would accept this. They have a vision of an equal rights feminism which says that if women are equal now, she can cope with having her book edited by men. I kept saying: The point is that men have not been sexually harassed at work, they don't understand what those processes are, they don't have those gut feelings, so that whereas a woman writing the book could go overboard with emotion at a certain point, another woman could recognise that and tell her, and be accepted. If a man said the same thing she'd probably say: 'Well, what the fuck do *you* know about it?' I think the lack of sensitivity on that point highlights for me where that struggle has to go on. It's not only talking about the hierarchy in the office or equal pay, it's actually talking about being prepared to acknowledge that women's liberation is a revolutionary movement which has as its central core the autonomy of women and the validity of women's experience of oppression, which men cannot understand or participate in, because they have not experienced it. They may indeed be guilty of causing that oppression themselves."

A lot of readers do not realise how vital the editorial role is, how much moving round and chucking out and control an editor can have over the eventual shape of a book, although their name practically never appears on the cover. The editor is usually chosen by the publishing house, and although a good editor should deal fairly with manuscripts they disagree with, if the author feels vulnerable — which is especially likely with a female author and a male editor — they are caught once again in a power relationship where they lose control over their work. We know of a number of women authors who have suffered

severely in this way at the hands of male editors at various publishing
houses, although we realise that male editors can also be supportive and
look at a manuscript dispassionately. We would like to plead for women
authors to campaign to be edited by sympathetic women wherever they
are published, but especially at socialist houses. This form of political
solidarity is one way of increasing the employment of properly
qualified women, as well as improving the quality and conditions of
your work. Manuscripts have been taken away from publishers who
would not provide a woman editor, but we realise the vulnerability of
this situation, too — you have to feel reasonably confident that you
can get it published elsewhere.

How far can feminists in these radical publishers make a difference?
Would it be better if we just encouraged feminist publishers rather than
trying to make headway in what is basically a sexist set-up in left publishers?

"The contradiction that's troubled me since I started there is that we
don't have a feminist publisher in this country to publish the sort of
political books that I am interested in. Perhaps that is unfair, because
maybe the books are not being written, or maybe the feminist publishers have tried to commission them and can't find anybody to
do it, or maybe they just haven't got the money and feel they won't
sell. What I am thinking of is the analytic book, of current politics
and debate, from a feminist perspective. For whatever reason, I
haven't seen books coming from the feminist publishers like that yet.
So that leaves you in the position where a feminist has written a
good book and if she takes it to a socialist publisher, well it's good
for the woman, and it may be good for the Movement, but it's also
good for the socialist publisher. Now do I *want* it to be good for
them? That is at the core of all the contradictory feelings that I
have.

As a publisher, are you radical only because of *what* you publish,
or is the way you publish it also important? What about your everyday treatment of your women authors, your female employees, not
to mention every woman in the world? But then again, suppose a
woman walks into a bookshop and buys that book, which is the one
that changes her life, would it have been worth the fact that it had
been published by someone who would treat her really badly if he
ever met her?"

None of us would be involved in conveying the written word to other
people if we did not believe books to be a vital accessory to political
activity, but books alone are not enough. It is the height of intellectual
arrogance to seriously believe that you can gain revolutionary consciousness and make the revolution happen through reading. At its
most extreme this is expressed in terms of books being specifically
aimed at those who are perceived as revolutionary 'leaders'. If you
believe profoundly enough that publishing the right book is primarily
how you bring about change, then your priority is indeed the book, and
your employees' conditions of work are of little or no importance. As
the recession deepens our radical brothers use it as an excuse whenever
feminists complain. However, the radical booktrade, and especially the

feminist part of it, is one sector that is surviving relatively well, so we shall be around and fighting for a while yet.

* In this chapter, although all quotes are genuine we have used fictitious names and changed minor details to preserve anonymity.

Bibliography

Arnold, June Feminist Presses and Feminist Politics, in *Quest: A Feminist Quarterly*, vol. 3, no. 1, 1976, pp. 18-26.

BBC Transcript of 'The Hype', *The Risk Business*, broadcast 14.5.80.

Braithwaite, Brian and Barrell, Joan *The Business of Women's Magazines*, Associated Business Press, 1979.

Christmas, Linda Miss Print and the Unions, *The Guardian*, 9.9.80.

Feminist Archive Information Sheet No. 1, 1980.

Hamill, Frances Some Unconventional Women Before 1800: Printers, Booksellers, and Collectors (separate from the Papers of the Bibliographical Society of America), vol. 49, Fourth Quarter, 1955.

Hunt, Felicity *Women Workers in the Book-Binding and Printing Trade 1795-1914 — with special reference to London*, University of Essex unpublished M.A. thesis 1980.

Joan, Polly and Chesman, Andrea *Guide to Women's Publishing*, Dustbooks, 1978.

Jordan and Sons Surveys, *Book publishing*, Jordan Biannual.

Lane, Michael and Booth, Jerry *Books and Publishers: Commerce against Culture in Post-war Britain*, Lexington Books, 1980.

Leonard, Diana Is Feminism more Complex than the WLM Realises? in *Feminist Practice*, 1979. (Available from In Theory Press, c/o Reema, 36-8 Lexington St, London W1.)

News From Neasden Special Issue on Women and Publishing, no. 11, Spring 1979. (Available from 12, Fleet Road, London NW3.)

NUJ Equality Working Party *Non-Sexist Code of Practice for Book Publishing*, 1975.

Orwell, George Pamphlet Literature, in *The Collected Essays, Journalism and Letters of George Orwell, vol. 2*, ed. by Sonia Orwell and Ian Angus, Penguin Books, 1970.

Print Why the Association has Launched a Major New Recruitment Drive to Welcome White-Collar Workers, NGA, November 1979.

Pritchard, A. and Doughan, D. Access to the Literature on Women, in *Assistant Librarian*, February 1979.

Shepherd, Leslie *The History of Street Literature*, David & Charlesss, 1973.

Sinclair, Peter *Radical Publishing as a Part of the Industry as a Whole*, Minority Press Group Conference Paper, 1980.

Sissons, R. and Kennedy, S. The Growth of the New Radicals, in *The Bookseller*, 22.3.80.

Smith, Keith *Marketing for Small Publishers*, Inter-Action Inprint, 1980.

Spender, Dale The Gatekeepers: A Feminist Critique of Academic Publishing, in *Doing Feminist Research*, ed. by H. Roberts, Routledge & Kegan Paul, 1981.

Sykes, Paul *The Public Library in Perspective*, Clive Bingley, 1979.

Walbe, J. and Davison, W. The Women's Research and Resources Centre, in *Assistant Librarian*, February 1979.

Ward, M.L. *Readers and Library Users*, Library Association, 1977.

Ward, Patricia Layzell Access to the Literature on Equal Opportunity: The Equal Opportunities Information Centre, in *Assistant Librarian*, February 1979.

West, Celeste and Wheat, Valerie *The Passionate Perils of Publishing*, Booklegger Press, 1978. (Available from Booklegger Press, 555 29th Street, San Francisco 94131, USA $5.)

White, Cynthia L. *Women's Magazines 1693-1968*, Michael Joseph, 1970.

Women's Liberation Bookbus *Women's Liberation Bookbus*, 1980.

Writers' and Artists' Yearbook, A. & C. Black.

Appendix I

DIRECTORY OF WOMEN'S LIBERATION NEWSLETTERS, MAGAZINES AND JOURNALS

Covering Scotland, Wales, England and Ireland

When writing to any of these periodicals for information, please enclose an S.A.E. for their reply.

This list was compiled with the help of WIRES, who should have the most up to date information.

Women's Liberation Local Newsletters — all are for women only

Bath Feminist Newsletter
1 Walcot Parade
Bath
Avon

Birmingham Women's Liberation
Newsletter
Cath Hall
65 Prospect Road
Kings Heath
Birmingham

Bradford Women's Liberation Newsletter
2 Aireville Road
Frizinghall
Bradford

Brighton and Hove Women's Liberation
Newsletter
Women's Centre
Resources Centre
North Street
Brighton
Sussex

Bristol Women's Liberation Newsletter
Women's Centre
44 The Grove
Bristol 1

Cambridge Women's Liberation
Newsletter
Women's Centre
48 Eden Street
Cambridge

Edinburgh Women's Liberation
Newsletter
Women's Centre
61A Broughton Street
Edinburgh

Glasgow Women's Liberation Newsletter
57 Miller Street
Glasgow 1

Glastonbury Thorn
Flat 1
Rhiston
Streer Road
Glastonbury, Somerset

Haringey Women's Centre Newsletter
40 Turnpike Lane
London N8

Hull Collective Newsletter
40 Middleton Street
Hull

Lancaster Women's Liberation
Newsletter
The Plough
Moor Lane
Lancaster

Leeds Women's Liberation Newsletter
Corner Bookshop
Woodhouse Lane
Leeds

Leicester Women's Liberation
Newsletter
50 Eastleigh Road
Leicester

London Women's Liberation Newsletter
c/o A Woman's Place
48 William IV Street
London WC2

Manchester Women's Liberation
Newsletter
36 Whitechapel Road
Manchester 20

Merseyside Women's Liberation
Newsletter
Women's Centre
Rialto Community Centre
Upper Parliament St
Liverpool 8

Women's Liberation Local Newsletters — all are for women only contd

Norwich Women's Liberation
  Newsletter
14/16 Argyle St
Norwich

Nottingham Women's Liberation
  Newsletter
32a Shakespeare St
Nottingham

Oxford Women's Liberation Newsletter
35-37 Cowley Road
Oxford

Plymouth Newsletter
Women's Centre
Virginia House
Palace St
Plymouth

Sheffield Women's Liberation Newsletter
8 Goodwin
Sheffield 8

York Women's Liberation Newsletter
32a Parliament St
York

Newsletters and Magazines that have national circulation and/or deal with particular areas of interest.

AIMS Newsletter
Christine Burley
Lansdowne House
5 Lansdowne Square
Hove, Sussex
    Association for Improvements
    in Maternity Services

Anarcha-Feminist Newsletter
Sisterwrite
190 Upper St
London N1
    Women only

Bean Saor
Resource Centre
52 Broadway
Belfast
    Women against Imperialism newsletter

Breaking Chains
ALRA
88a Islington High St
London N1
    Abortion Law Reform Association

Catcall
37 Wortley Rd
London E6
    Feminist theory magazine
    Women only

Christian Feminists Newsletter
Shelagh Robinson
22 Foreshore
Pepys Estate
London SE8

The Collective Fund Newsletter
Rights for Women, NCCL
186 Kings Cross Rd
London WC1

Crystal Crone
108 Albion Drive
London E8
    Women's science fiction

Drastic Measures
Room 265
27 Clerkenwell Close
London EC1
    Rock Against Sexism

Feminism and Non-Violence Newsletter
168 Hamilton Rd
Longsight
Manchester 13

Feminist Arts Newsletter (FAN)
79 Blenheim Road
Birmingham 13

Feminist Review
65 Manor Rd
London N16
    Theoretical journal

Feminists Against Sexual Terrorism
  Newsletter (FAST)
37 Chestnut Avenue
Leeds 6
    Women only

Fightback (against the cuts)
30 Camden Rd
London NW1

For the Likes of Us
Julia Tant
3 Kestrel Avenue
London SE24
    Working class women's newsletter
    Women only

FOWAAD
Black Women's Centre
41A Stockwell Green
London SW9
    Newsletter of the Organisation of
    Women of Asian and African Descent

Girls Newsletter
Camden Girls Centre Project
4 Caversham Rd
London NW5
    Women only

Insist — Brum Women's Paper
Peace Centre
Moor St
Ringway, Birmingham 4

Insist — Brum Women's Paper
Peace Centre
Moor St
Ringway, Birmingham 4

**International Contraception, Abortion
and Sterilisation Campaign Newsletter**
from NAC
374 Grays Inn Rd
London WC1

Link
Women's Magazine of the Communist
    Party
16 St John St
London EC1

London Lesbian Newsletter
Sheril Berkovitch
66 Marchmont St
London WC1

Manchester Women's Paper
30 Clothorn Rd
Didsbury
Manchester 20

Manushi
147 Grove Lane
London SE5
    An Indian feminist journal available
    in Britain

Matriarchy News
c/o 190 Upper St
London N1
    Women only

Merseyside Women's Paper
Sue Ryrie
18 Hawarden Avenue
Liverpool 17

M/F
22 Chepstow Crescent
London W11
    Theoretical journal, marxist feminist
    perspective

Msprint
Nina Woodcock
74 Arklay Street
Dundee

**National Abortion Campaign (NAC)
    Newsletter**
374 Grays Inn Rd
London WC1

National Childcare Campaign Newsletter
Surrey Docks Childcare Project
Dockland Settlement
Redriff Rd
London SE16

Nessie
1 Ritchie Place
Edinburgh
    Scottish Radical/Revolutionary
    Feminist Newsletter
    Women only

**Northern Ireland Women's Aid
    Newsletter**
12 Orchard St
Derry
N Ireland
    Circulates within WAF

Red Rag
207 Sumatra Rd
London NW6 1PF
    Marxist feminist magazine

**Revolutionary/Radical Feminist
    Newsletter**
17 Kensington Terrace
Leeds 6
    Women only

Rhiannon
35 Commercial Rd
Pill, Newport
Gwent

ROW Bulletin (Rights of Women)
374 Grays Inn Rd
London WC1

Sappho
Basement
20 Dorset Sq
London NW1
    Lesbian magazine

Scarlet Women
5 Washington Terrace
North Shields
Tyne and Wewar
    Newsletter of the Socialist-feminist
    current

Scottish Women's Aid Newsletter
11 St Colme St
Edinburgh

Sequel
BM Sequel
London WC1V 6XX
    For isolated lesbians

Shocking Pink
4 Essex Rd
London W4
    Young women's magazine

Sour Cream
c/o 190 Upper Street
London N1
    Bi-monthly collection of feminist
    cartoons

Spare Rib
27 Clerkenwell Close
London EC1

Spinster
40 St Lawrence Terrace
London W10
    Feminist literary magazine

Welsh Women's Aid Newsletter
Incentive House
Adam Street
Cardiff
Wales
    Circulates within WAF

Wicca
'Ensa' Tivoli Road
Dun Laoghaire
Eire

WIRES Newsletter
32a Shakespeare St
Nottingham
    National Women's Liberation
    internal newsletter
    Women only

Women and Education Newsletter
14 St Brendans Rd
Withington
Manchester 20

Women and Manual Trades Newsletter
40 Dale St
London W4

Women and Writing Newsletter
Janet Batsleer/Rebecca O'Rourke
Adult Education Centre
37 Harrow Rd
Middlesborough
Cleveland

Women in Action
Box 2, Sisterwrite
190 Upper St
London N1
    Women in Trade Unions

Women in Eastern Europe Newsletter
CREES
The University
Birmingham 15

Women in Entertainments Newsletter
11 Acklam Rd
London W10

Women Matter
Falkirk Women's Aid
6 Lesley Place
Kerse Lane
Falkirk
    Central Scottish Women's Aid
    Newsletter

Women on Wheels
31 Sisters Avenue
London SW11
    Women bikers newsletter
    Women only

Women Speaking
Esther Hodge
70 Westmount Rd
London SE9

Women with Children Newsletter
Sylvia Newman
41 Beech Avenue
Sanderstead
Surrey

Women's Aid Federation (England)
    Newsletter
374 Grays Inn Rd
London WC1
    Circulates within WAFE

Women's Media Action Bulletin
10 Cambridge Terrace Mews
London NW1

Women's Research and Resources
Centre Newsletter
190 Upper St
London N1

Women's Studies International Quarterly
Dale Spender (Editor)
Flat 4, Rosetti House
Flood Street
London SW3 5TG

Women's Studies Newsletter
Carolyn Brown
176 Hagley Rd
Stourbridge DY8 2JN

Women's View
30 Gardiner Place
Dublin 1
Eire
   Women's magazine of Sinn Fein
   The Workers Party

Women's Voice
PO Box 82
London E2
   Women's magazine of the Socialist
   Workers Party

Womenergy
24 Ranclife Rd
London E6
   Women against nukes newsletter
   Women only

Working with Girls Newsletter
NAYC
PO Box 1, Blackburn House
Bond Gate
Nuneaton
Warks

Appendix II

Useful organisations

*indicates that this organisation is discussed in the text.

The information section of the Spare Rib Women's Liberation Diary was very helpful for compiling this list.

All-Women printers and typesetters

Bradford Printshop
127 Thornton Road,
Bradford 1
    Silkscreen postcards, T shirts,
    posters, etc

* Dark Moon Typesetters,
43 All Saints Road
London W11
01 221 4331

* Moss Side Community Press
21A Princess Road
Manchester 14
061 226 7115

* Onlywomen Press
38 Mount Pleasant
London WC1
01 837 0596

* Red Lion Setters
22 Brownlow Mews
London WC1
01 405 4498

* See Red Women's Workshop
16A Illife Yard
off Crampton Street
London SE17
01 701 8314
    Silkscreen posters

Sheffield Women's Printing Co-op
Commonground Resources Centre
87 The Wicker
Sheffield 3
0742 738572
    Offset-litho up to B 4 size.
    Serves mainly South Yorkshire

* Women in Print
16A Illiffe Yard
off Crampton Street
London SE17
01 701 8314

Feminist Publishers

Arlen House (the women's press)
2 Grange Park
Baldoyle
Dublin 13
Eire
Dublin 392520

Falling Wall Press
9 Lawford Street
Old Market
Bristol 2
0272 559230

* Onlywomen Press — see above

* Sheba Feminnist Publishers
488 Kingsland Road
London E8
01 254 1590

* Stramullion
43 Candlemaker Row
Edinburgh 1
Scotland

*Virago Press
Ely House
37 Dover Street
London W1
01 499 9716

* The Women's Press
124 Shoreditch High Street
London E1
01 729 5257

Feminist information, resource centres, and meeting places

* A Woman's Place
48 William IV Street
London WC2
01 836 6081
    Women's Liberation information
    and meeting centre with bookstall

* Equal Opportunities Commission
Information Centre
Overseas House
Quay Street
Manchester 3
061 833 9244

* Fawcett Library
City of London Polytechnic
Old Castle Street
London E1
01 283 1030

* Feminist Archive
Temporary Address
c/o Sue Cuthbert
8 St Saviour's Terrace
Larkhall
Bath
Avon
Bath 334048

* Sisterwrite Bookshop
190 Upper Street
London N1
01 226 9782

* Wires
32A Shakespeare Street
Nottingham
0602 411475
    Women's Liberation national
    information service

* Women's Arts Alliance
10 Cambridge Terrace Mews
London NW1
01 935 1841
    Feminist cultural activities with
    bookstall, cafe and exhibition space

* Women's Research and Resources
Centre
190 Upper Street
London N1
01 359 5773
    Information on feminist research,
    library and reading room

Women's organisations and campaigns

AFFIRM — Alliance for Fair Images and
Representation in the Media
c/o WAA
10 Cambridge Terrace Mews
London NW1

Black Women in Media
18 Western Court
245 Carlton Vale
London NW6

CISSY — Campaign to Impede Sexual
Stereotyping in the Young
177 Gleneldon Road
London SW16
01 677 2411
    Covers books, comics, toys, TV

Equality Working Party (of NUJ)
Acorn House
314 Grays Inn Road
London WC1

Irish — Sheffield Women's Photography
Group
Dais Cliffe
70 Edgedale Road
Sheffield

Northern Irish Women in Media
c/o Just Books
7 Winetavern Street
Belfast 1

Society of Women Writers and
Journalists
c/o 45 Basildon Court
Devonshire Street
London W1
    Holds monthly meetings for
    professional writers. Established in
    1894.

WAMM — Women Against Media Myths
c/o Bristol Women's Centre
44 The Grove
Bristol 1

Women and Graphics Network
c/o Insist
Peace Centre
Moor Street
Ringway
Birmingham 4

Women in Libraries
Sherry Jasperson
8 Hill Road
London NW8
01 486 5811 (work)

Women in Media
Flat 10
59 Drayton Gardens
London SW10

* Women in Publishing
Flat 2, 40 Menelik Road
London NW2

Women Printers' Group
c/o Cromer Street Women's Centre
90 Cromer Street
London WC1

* Women's Liberation Bookbus
c/o A Woman's Place
48 William IV Street
London WC2

Trade Unions

Artists Union
9 Poland St
London W1
01 437 1984

ASTMS (Publishing Branch)
10 Jamestown Rd
London NW1
01 267 4422

* National Graphical Association
63-67 Bromham Rd ·
Bedford MK40 2AG
0234 51521

* National Union of Journalists
314 Gray's Inn Rd
London WC1
01 278 7916
        Has large active book branch

* NATSOPA (National Society of
Operative Printers, Graphical & Media
Personnel)
13 Borough Rd
London SE1
01 928 1481

Society of Authors
84 Drayton Gardens
London SW10
01 373 6642
        Non-TUC affiliated union

* SLADE (Society of Lithographic
Artists, Designers, Engravers and Process
Workers)
55 Clapham Common South Side
London SW4
01 720 6551

* SOGAT (Society of Graphical and
Allied Trades)
London Rd
Hadleigh
Essex
Southend on Sea 553131

Theatre Writers' Union
Delegate Commission
c/o 9 Fitzroy Sq
London W1

* Writers' Guild of Great Britain
430 Edgware Rd
London W2
01 723 8074
        TUC affiliated union

Mixed Radical Organisations

Children's Rights Workshop
4 Aldebert Terrace
London SW8
        Produces Children's Books Bulletin

Federation of Radical Booksellers
York Community Books
73 Walmgate
York
0904 37355

* Federation of Worker Writers
Ken Worpole
76 Carysfort Rd
London N16

* Grass Roots Bookshop
1 Newton St
Manchester 1
061 236 3112

* PDC (Southern Distribution and
        Full Time Distribution)
Albion Yard, Balfe Street,
London N1.
01-837 1460

* Scottish & Northern Books (PDC)
45/47 Niddry Street
Edinburgh
031 557 0133

and

4th Floor
18 Granby Row
Manchester 1
061 228 3903

The Radical Bookseller
265 Seven Sisters Road
London N4
01 802 8773
monthly listing of new titles,
including feminist ones

Socialist Bookfair
Eve Barker
265 Seven Sisters Rd
London N4
01 802 6145
Held annually in London in the
autumn

Third World Publications
151 Stratford Rd
Birmingham 11
021 773 6572
Promotion and distribution

* Ultra Violet Enterprises
25 Horsell Rd
London N5
01 607 4463
Promotion and publicity of feminist
and radical literature

Other Useful Addresses

Arts Council of Great Britain
105 Piccadilly
London W1
01 629 9495
Can give you address of your
Regional Arts Association

Independent Publishers Guild
52 Chepstow Rd
London W2
01 727 0919

The National Book League
45 East Hill
Wandsworth
London SW18
01 870 9055

*** Printing and Publishing Industry
Training Board**
Merit House
Edgware Rd
London NW9
01 205 0162

FORTHCOMING
5   News Ltd: Developing Alternative Forms of Journalism by Brian Whittaker

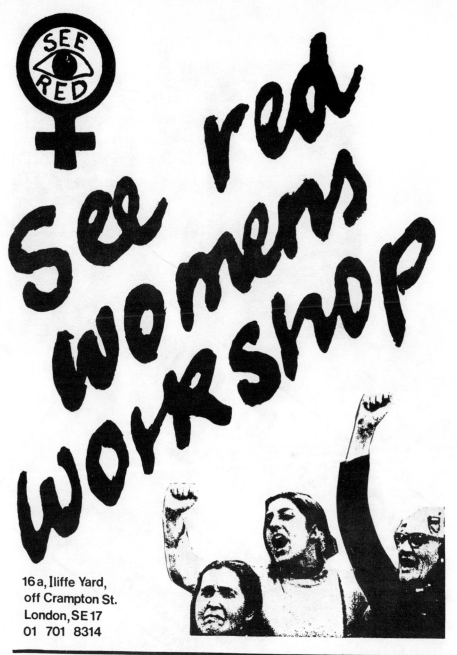

See red
womens
workshop

16a, Iliffe Yard,
off Crampton St.
London, SE 17
01 701 8314

We design and print feminist posters and cards (send large sae + 20p for catalogue).

We screenprint posters and t-shirts for meetings and events etc. at very reasonable rates.